Confidence
Boosters

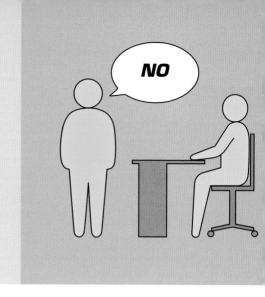

10 steps
to beating
self-doubt

CONFIDENCE

Confidence
Boosters

Martin Perry

I will win

hamlyn

A Pyramid Paperback

First published in Great Britain in 2005 by
Hamlyn, a division of Octopus Publishing Group Ltd
2–4 Heron Quays, London E14 4JP

Text copyright © Martin Perry 2005

Design copyright © Octopus Publishing Group Ltd
2005

This material was previously published as
Confidence Booster Workout

ISBN 0 600 61323 2
EAN 9780600613237

A CIP catalogue record for this book is available
from the British Library

Printed and bound in China

10 9 8 7 6 5 4 3 2 1

CONTENTS

Introduction 6

STEP 1 *Learning all about confidence* 8

STEP 2 *How to combat negative influences* 16

STEP 3 *Overcoming fear of failure* 24

STEP 4 *How to say no* 42

STEP 5 *Overcoming self-sabotage* 58

STEP 6 *Learning to cope* 70

STEP 7 *Social confidence* 78

STEP 8 *Making speeches and presentations* 90

STEP 9 *Unfortunate comparison* 100

STEP 10 *Having confidence in common situations* 112

Confidence-boosting exercise programme 126

Conclusion 139

Index 140

Acknowledgements 144

INTRODUCTION

Having confidence can be the vital passport to success in your personal and professional life. Confidence enables you to take on new challenges, to trust yourself in difficult situations, to go beyond your perceived limits, to tackle things you have never done before and to make full use of your natural talent and capability. Confidence gives you the courage not to worry about the consequences of failure. The hallmark of all truly confident people is that they focus on what they can do, and about the positive outcomes they will achieve, rather than worrying about what they can't do, and what might go wrong. Without confidence, life's challenges can seem insurmountable. Confidence provides the vigour to tackle these challenges.

LOSS OF CONFIDENCE

Once confidence has been lost, doubt and uncertainty prevail. The unconfident person gets into a cycle of behaviour that becomes increasingly difficult to break. Fear of failure leads to indecision, which leads to further self-doubt. Lost confidence can cause you, for example, to:

The good news is that lost confidence is not lost for ever – it has simply been overlaid by self-doubt.

- *avoid calling someone for a date, in case you are rejected*

- *blame others when things go wrong, rather than learning from your mistakes*

- *struggle to make clear-cut decisions in case you get them wrong*

- *avoid applying for jobs you want, because of the fear of being interviewed.*

Your natural confidence is there inside you at all times

We are all born with a degree of self-confidence

Introduction

REGAINING YOUR CONFIDENCE

The aim of this book is to help you break out of the negative cycle of self-doubt and enter into a positive cycle of increased confidence, success and happiness. The book provides key insights into why we lose confidence, in order to provide better understanding of why your confidence has disappeared, and these are supported by simple, practical exercises that will enable you to start rebuilding your confidence straight away.

The exercises are drawn from the work I have done as a Confidence Coach with clients over the last seven years. Many of these people had forgotten what it felt like to be confident. For them self-doubt had become a way of life. However the majority of them have now got their confidence back and are taking on new challenges with a renewed belief in themselves. They are living testimony to the self-fulfilling motto: 'It doesn't have to be this way.'

PHONE A FRIEND

Why not get a friend or relative to work with you on some of the exercises? This is the next best thing to having a professional coach. Choose someone you can trust and will enjoy working with. It will make the process more enjoyable if they also want to

build up their confidence. Using this system means that you have someone who you are accountable to other than yourself.

Agree to call each other on a weekly basis to check on each other's progress. This will keep the confidence-building process moving. In your conversations, you can ask such questions as:

- **What success have you had in the last week?**

- **What setbacks have you suffered?**

- **What did you learn from those setbacks?**

- **What would you like to achieve this week?**

- **What support do you need to make good that achievement?**

To have confidence is as natural as being able to walk or talk. Those who regain their confidence after having lost it value it even more than those who have always had it. To rebuild confidence takes courage and desire. I hope that this book will make this journey much easier for you.

7

LEARNING ALL ABOUT
CONFIDENCE

Before you can start to improve your levels of self-confidence, it is important for you to determine how confident you are now, and to learn about what confidence is and how it manifests itself in everyday life. This step will help you to assess your initial level of confidence and give you an appreciation of how the techniques outlined in this book could help you.

 TEST: HOW CONFIDENT ARE YOU?

To assess your current state of confidence, for each of the 10 statements below rate yourself on a scale of 1–10 (where 1 means you agree strongly with the statement, and 10 means you disagree strongly with it).

1 I am scared of saying no to others in case they dislike me.

2 I feel the need to be accepted by agreeing with everyone, regardless of whether I actually agree with them or not.

3 I don't give myself the allowance and freedom to get things wrong and make mistakes.

4 I don't forgive myself for the mistakes I make.

5 I often think to myself 'I am not good enough.'

6 I often compare myself unfavourably with others.

7 I feel riddled with guilt when I am tempted to do things that I want to do.

8 I am frightened of the idea of achieving success.

9 I find it difficult to make clear-cut decisions.

10 I am often too hard on myself.

YOUR SCORE

Under 30: lack of confidence is really holding you back.

30–70: you need to work on your confidence using the exercises in this book.

Over 70: you are well on your way to having the confidence you need to succeed.

WHAT IS CONFIDENCE?

Being confident means feeling positive about what you can do, and not worrying about what you can't do, but having the will to learn. Self-confidence is the oil that smoothly turns the wheels of the relationship between you, your capability – that is, your natural talents, skills and potential – and your ability to make good that capability.

OUTER OR 'ENFORCED' CONFIDENCE

There is a preconception that confident people are loud, bold, extrovert types who can handle any personal and professional situation that they face with the minimum of fuss and the maximum of certainty. The truth, however, is that those people who are the greatest self-promoters about who they are and what they do are often wearing a 'mask' of confidence. This is the outer expression of the person's behaviour, which may hide an inner fear or uncertainty from which they are trying to escape.

This is not real confidence. It is 'enforced' confidence, and they are 'confidence enforcers'. They wear the mask of confidence to ensure that they remain in control of situations, and this is born out of the fear of not being in control. They have discovered that the more control they have over others the greater respect they are afforded. A confidence enforcer's need for control over people and situations arises from the fact that they were at one time or another made to feel small inside by other people. They realize that the feeling of being small will not get them very far in the world, so they have

Less confident people are afraid of being hurt and having their confidence damaged even more

developed an over-inflated self-view, so that they can feel big and make others feel small.

WHY IS SUCH BEHAVIOUR PERCEIVED AS CONFIDENCE?

The answer is simply because confidence enforcers don't give off a hint of self-doubt. They seem so sure of themselves. 'How could I possibly be wrong?' they seem to suggest. They don't want to be seen to be wrong or not in control, because they feed off others' perceptions of them as someone who is always right and in control.

People with low amounts of confidence can often be intimidated by a confidence enforcer, since the enforcer appears hard to stand up to because of the amount of power and control they seem to have at their disposal. They haven't got enough inner strength at their disposal to handle the confidence enforcer. The enforcer feeds off this fear, because it is a way for them to get some recognition and find a place and role in the world. School bullies and tyrannical bosses are good examples of this.

INNER OR 'TRUE'
CONFIDENCE

True confidence is different; it is a 'quiet' state and begins on the inside. In this context, 'quiet' means that there is no interference upon the natural state of affairs. No background noise, no doubts, no comparison with others, no fear of failure, no worry about what others are thinking – this is the inner state of confidence. There is the 'golden triangle' between the person, their capability and the moment.

Have you ever observed a leading professional – perhaps a dancer, musician, athlete or surgeon – at work? You will notice that, when they are performing or operating at their very peak, they exude a sense of quietness and authority. What we are witnessing is the state of no interference between the person and their capability; this allows them to perform at the peak of their ability, because there is nothing preventing them from doing so.

In the presence of confidence, doubt can't exist

YOU ARE CONFIDENT

YOUR CONFIDENCE IS INCREASED

PEOPLE HAVE CONFIDENCE IN YOU

THE CYCLE OF CONFIDENCE

In the presence of such people you have complete confidence that they will do what they say they will do. For example, if you love to watch great dancers in action, you will pay to see a leading ballet company, because the individuals in that company are dedicated to the art of dance. They are confident dancers. They dance with confidence. When they dance, their confidence in themselves causes the audience to have complete confidence in them, which adds to the confidence of the dancers ... and thus the cycle flows.

ZERO INTERFERENCE REQUIRES:

- **No doubts**

- **No comparison with others**

- **No fear of failure**

- **No worry about what others are thinking**

If your boss asks you to lock up the office when you finish work, and you do this job in a complete way on a regular basis, then your boss will have increased confidence in you. Knowing this, you will complete the task with increased confidence, which further cements the boss's confidence in you, and so the confidence cycle flows. If a garage does excellent work on your car, you are inclined to recommend them to others, because you have complete confidence in their ability to fix cars. You have confidence in them because of the confidence they have in what they do; as a result others have confidence in the mechanics because of your confidence in them and their own confidence in you.

You cause other people to have confidence in you, as well as having confidence in yourself and confidence in others. You can give others reason to have confidence in you.

THE NATURE OF CONFIDENCE

To understand more about the inner nature of confidence, think about some similar words and expressions. The word confidence is related to the terms 'confide' and 'confidential'. When you confide in someone, you permit them to know information that you trust they will not pass on to others. That person becomes a 'confidant', because you have confidence in their ability to keep a confidence. Again, when information is deemed to be confidential, or something is told 'in confidence', it indicates that it remains secret and its contents are not to be disclosed. If the confidant were to break that trust, they would betray your confidence.

So a state of confidence is one of being able to trust your own capability. You have been gifted this capability of confidence.

Zero interference means that nothing comes between the person and their capability

THE CONFIDENCE
SPECTRUM

People vary in their self-view and outward manner, ranging from arrogance, at one end of the spectrum, through the well-balanced state of confidence, to low self-esteem at the other extreme. In addition, there are a couple of intermediate states, namely supreme confidence and self-doubt. You need to know about all of these before you can start to improve your own confidence levels.

ARROGANCE

Arrogant people assume that they will suc-ceed at a given task. They have had success before. It is natural for them to think that suc-cess will continue to come their way. Arrogant people are disliked because they believe that they have a divine right to con-tinued success. When a politician or business magnate falls from grace, it can very often cause great delight in others because their assumption of continued power has been shattered. The assumption is in fact a belief that what was before will always be.

I always win

Arrogance, or the bloated self-view that success is permanent, means that the per-son often becomes so consumed with the sense of their own self-importance that they are no longer able to attract continued suc-cess. With every success their ego grows until there is no living space for anything else except themselves.

supreme confidence + assumption = arrogance

Arrogance is at the top end of the confidence spectrum

SUPREME CONFIDENCE

Supremely confident people have no doubts that they will succeed. They focus on their strengths and have a keen sense of what they want, but allied to this is a powerful will – a hunger and desire to succeed 'come what may'. Each success that they attract confirms their self-worth. Their hunger and desire prevents them from becoming assumptive about success. These are the people who set the trends and break the records for others to follow. The supremely confident person believes with every cell of their being that they will succeed, but if for some reason they don't it rarely diminishes their strong and powerful self-view that they will succeed next time.

This type of person invariably learns wisely from their failures, and it will take a major shock and reverse to sever their line of trust between themselves and their capability. Such supremely confident people might, for example, be millionaires who for some reason lose their personal fortune and become bankrupt, only to rebuild their personal wealth through a new venture.

There is a very fine line, however, between supreme confidence and arrogance. Sometimes when a person becomes too familiar with success they cross this thin dividing line. Too much success can lead to arro-

I should win

gance, because the person has become so used to success that they take it for granted that success will continue to occur.

The test for the supremely confident person is: can they continue to keep renewing their relationship with success and remaining hungry for success? It is the absence of familiarity with success that keeps the supremely confident person on the right side of the line.

confidence + belief = supreme confidence

CONFIDENCE

Confident people prepare to attract the outcome they seek. They focus on the strengths that they will bring to any given situation. They have had success, and draw on those previous successes to inform them that they can attract success again. Their well of success is deep and their line of trust between themselves and their capability is strong.

natural capability + trust = confidence

I will win

SELF-DOUBT

Self-doubters tend to focus on all the things that will or could go wrong. They worry about the potential negative outcomes, because past evidence suggests that they will have a negative outcome. They focus on their own doubts rather than their own strengths. Their self-doubts are stronger than their ability to focus on their strengths, because of the impact that 'failure' has had on them before. They feel the pain of previous failure and are worried of having more 'failure' to experience. They know that they have the ability to take on the situation they face, but nevertheless these doubts still hold sway. The line of trust between themselves and their capability has been disconnected.

I'll probably lose

capability – trust = self-doubt

LOW SELF-ESTEEM

Self-esteem means the value that a person places upon who they are and what they do. People with low self-esteem feel that it is not worth even trying to succeed, because they will fail anyway. Their opinion of themselves is low because they have resigned themselves to playing the role of the loser or the victim. They believe that others win and succeed in life, but they don't. They become trapped in this cycle.

No point bothering

Where there is low self-esteem, confidence needs careful rebuilding. This can be achieved through the person sampling small, achievable successes, so that they begin to have a relationship with success and thus with the self-confidence that says 'I can succeed.'

natural capability – trust – self-worth = low self-esteem

📖 EXERCISE: ASSESS YOURSELF

Having read through the above categories, try to assess which one best describes your own level of confidence. If you feel that you are veering towards the arrogant end of the scale, perhaps you should look to moderate your self-view and thereby improve your relations with other people. If, however, you find yourself at the lower end of the confidence spectrum, you should definitely benefit from the confidence-boosting advice that is given throughout the rest of this book.

FIND CONFIDENCE
IN EVERYDAY LIFE

A very simple way to begin to gain confidence is to think about examples of where confidence exists in everyday life. The purpose of this is that you become a confidence 'researcher', and thereby start to think in a more positive way than maybe you have been used to.

THE CONFIDENCE MAGNET

To attract confidence you must have confidence. If you don't have confidence, you must go and 'collect' some, thus becoming a confidence 'magnet'. Here are some examples to get you started.

**SUCCESS
WEALTH
PROMOTION**

- *The confidence that a tightrope walker has in their ability to stay on the rope.*
- *The confidence that reliable people inspire in others around them that the job will get done.*
- *The confidence we have that the sun will rise and set tomorrow.*
- *The confidence we have in our bodies' ability to do those things that we* *generally don't have to think much about, such as breathing or that we will heal when we cut ourselves.*
- *The confidence a pilot has in the mechanics of his plane.*
- *The confidence of a child in the presence of his or her parents.*

EXERCISE: COLLECT EXAMPLES OF CONFIDENCE

Collect some examples from everyday life of where you can see confidence in action. Either write the examples down in a notebook or collect examples in picture form and create a collage. In this collage, place a picture of yourself to associate yourself with confidence. The purpose of this exercise is that, by collecting examples, you begin to become attracted to confidence by virtue of the fact that you are looking for it.

HOW TO COMBAT
NEGATIVE INFLUENCES

We are all born with a degree of natural confidence. This gives us the ability to do without even thinking all those things that we might now think of as automatic – breathing, smiling, sleeping, seeing, hearing, walking, talking, laughing and crying. It is only when we fear we might lose one of these 'innate' abilities that we realize how much they mean to us in our everyday living. Our natural confidence, however, is soon affected by negative influences.

NEGATIVE INFLUENCES

✪ *Blame and criticism*

✪ *Conformity*

✪ *Exclusion*

✪ *Competition*

✪ *Disappointment*

✪ *Perfectionism*

✪ *Dominance*

SEVEN MAJOR NEGATIVE INFLUENCES

In this step, each of the seven major negative influences is covered in turn, first giving you an insight into their nature and possible sources, and then pointing you towards positive ways of countering their effects.

BLAME AND CRITICISM

The twin influences of blame and criticism gradually eat away at your confidence. They can come from a number of sources.

Your parents

Perhaps you always received criticism from your parents, which can happen for the most unexpected reasons, for example the fact that you were born a girl and they had set their hearts on a boy, or vice versa, so that you will never meet their expectations. Maybe as a child you were clumsy, and so your parents constantly berated you for your clumsiness, which then put you under even

mistakes + blame = low confidence

greater pressure not to be clumsy, which of course made you even more clumsy.

Perhaps your parents held very high expectations for you, to compensate for what they were not able to achieve in their own lives. If you were unable to meet these high expectations, their disappointment in you turned to criticism. In the presence of criticism, it becomes very difficult to feel confident.

The workplace

Maybe you work for a boss or manager who never says an encouraging word, even when you do good work, so that you expect them to find fault with everything. Whenever you are called into their office, you presume it is because you have done something wrong. You work in an atmosphere of uncertainty, never sure if you are doing a good job, and with one eye over your shoulder for another negative comment about what you are doing.

Some companies believe that this way of working keeps staff on their toes. The thinking is that when the staff feel insecure they work harder to make sure they keep their jobs. It certainly does make the staff feel insecure, but there is little evidence to show

Criticism destroys confidence

that it makes them more confident and therefore more accomplished in their work.

If they want to retain a happy and confident workforce, good managers will always praise their staff for the things they have done well in the workplace, rather than always focusing on what they have not done well. They will call their staff into the office, sit them down and point out their successes. This gives the staff confidence in their bosses, as well as more confidence in themselves.

good work + encouragement = self-confidence

TOP 5 SYMPTOMS OF BLAME AND CRITICISM

1 **You think that everything that goes wrong is your fault.**
2 **You become highly sensitive to any criticism.**
3 **You expect to be told off whatever you do.**
4 **You blame yourself when things don't work out.**
5 **You dare not take risks in case you fail.**

Partners

Being constantly criticized by a partner can have very negative consequences on your confidence. Criticism eats away at your natural confidence, especially since you are more open and susceptible to those people who are close to you, and therefore are more deeply affected by their negative words. It may be that your partner has a 'perfect' view of what they want you to be like, and you don't fit this identikit picture. The gap between their 'perfect' partner imagery and the real you causes them to be critical of the things that you do that don't fit their image.

This state of affairs is very unsettling and creates a deep feeling of unease that will

Being bullied can have devastating effects on your self-confidence

make you think that whatever you do won't be good enough. All you ever hear about yourself are negative messages, and gradually these negative messages take root and you start to believe them. Eventually, you may even feel that you deserve the criticism.

CONFORMITY

Have you ever been in a room full of people and known the answer to a question, asked by a teacher or work colleague, but kept quiet

TOP 5 SYMPTOMS OF CONFORMITY

1 **You put off making decisions in case you are wrong.**
2 **You are timid and don't accept opportunities when they arise.**
3 **You judge yourself ('I'm stupid').**
4 **You try too hard to please others.**
5 **You make decisions because you think you should, rather than because you want to.**

in case you were wrong? This is probably because the last time you gave a wrong answer you were laughed at. If you are a sensitive person, the pain of this feeling of being laughed at may have been so great that you will make sure it never happens again.

Alternatively, your classmates or colleagues may have criticized you for always being right. It was not your fault that you knew the answer, but this reaction made you not want to be right, because of the criticism that would invite. You don't want to be excluded from your friends' circle, so you rein in your desire to participate fully in the class or meeting to avoid being regarded as either too bright or an idiot. The significance of this is that it damages the intimate feeling of trust between you and yourself.

opportunity – trust = remorse

You know the answer but you dare not say it. This leads to a state of contradiction in yourself, where you end up ignoring your instincts because they are not what everyone else is saying, feeling or thinking. Therefore you must be wrong. You ignore your gut feelings in case you are wrong, even though they often turn out to be right. This can lead to much regret and remorse, meaning that you dare not go out and do the things that you want to do in case you fail.

Another problem may be that we think it is too late to do the things that we want to do, such as learning to play a musical instrument, leaving our partners, sailing around the world or starting a new career. Our decision-making becomes influenced by what others do, rather than what our instincts and gut feelings are telling us to do.

EXCLUSION

You may have been overlooked for promotion at work, even though you were well qualified. Perhaps you were not allowed into a gang of friends, without explanation, even though you had done nothing wrong. Exclusion has a powerful impact upon confidence, because it creates a strong feeling of loneliness and the sense that you aren't good enough. You presume that there is something wrong with you, because this exclusion often comes without explanation or reason. The impact of loneliness makes you reflect inwardly and presume that you are at fault, since others have found reason to exclude you. This is an early symptom of self-sabotage, which will be explained later (see Step 6).

COMPETITION

From a very early age, we are introduced to the notion of competition. At school, we learn how to play competitive sports, and our academic performance is assessed and often compared with that of others. In adult life, we often encounter the same kind of thinking in our working environment.

TOP 5 SYMPTOMS OF EXCLUSION

1 You constantly 'suck up' to the decision-maker so that you can be included.
2 Your confidence state is one of uncertainty, because you don't know where you stand with other people.
3 You constantly experience the negative feeling that you are not good enough.
4 You feel resentment and jealousy that others get the opportunities and you don't.
5 You tend to make unfortunate comparisons (see Step 9) with those who are included.

TOP 5 SYMPTOMS OF COMPETITION

1 You compare yourself with others, often unfavourably.
2 You even start to doubt your own ability.
3 You put yourself under stress and pressure to succeed, when you are already trying as hard as you possibly can.
4 You find yourself wanting to impress and get approval and confirmation from others.
5 In extreme examples, you may even use stealing, deception, lying and cheating to get what you want, because the way that you usually do things does not achieve the desired result.

If you compete and don't win on a regular basis, you can develop the mindset that you will never achieve what you want. It is the mindset that says that someone else gets there first. You become accustomed to disappointment. This affects your confidence because of the contradiction between trying your best and not being rewarded for your efforts. You then expect not to win and develop a 'what's the point?' attitude.

DISAPPOINTMENT

Imagine that your boss has indicated you are in line for the next promotion that becomes available. You begin to imagine what this new job would be like – increased salary, responsibility commensurate with your capability, increased benefits. Then, when the job becomes available, for no apparent reason, and no explanation, your boss overlooks you and offers the job to someone else. All the expectancy that has been building up in you over the months turns to disappointment.

Disappointment can also materialize in personal relationships. Maybe you were due to marry the person you loved, when they broke off the relationship because they had fallen for someone else. Think how this disappointment might affect your confidence.

If you have experienced much disappointment in your life, this will eventually cause you to mistrust both others and yourself. Thus, you become wary of committing yourself in case disappointment happens again. You become cynical and don't believe what people tell you. Broken promises can have a major impact upon your ability to trust.

promises + disappointment = mistrust

PERFECTIONISM

The problem of perfectionism often stems from your parents, who may have set very high standards for you to live up to. This causes you to have extremely high standards

TOP 5 SYMPTOMS OF DISAPPOINTMENT

1 You expect things to go wrong, so you don't even bother trying.
2 You feel that you are not good enough for something good to happen to you.
3 You grow to fear hope, in case of being let down.
4 You mistrust when things go well, feeling that something is bound to go wrong.
5 You don't commit to relationships, for fear of being let down.

TOP 5 SYMPTOMS OF PERFECTIONISM

1 You think that failure is unacceptable.
2 You won't let other people see your mistakes.
3 You always anticipate and fear disapproval.
4 You have a constant craving for reassurance.
5 You criticize yourself for not being perfect.

and expectations for yourself and your own children, because your parents wanted you to do better. You may have received the message from this that other people value you for how much you have accomplished or achieved rather than for who you are. You may then measure yourself against what your parents were able to achieve. Perfectionism becomes a dominant influence rather than a liberating one, because you are not free to make mistakes. This affects your confidence, because you feel that you must do everything perfectly first time round.

DOMINANCE

Being bullied, at school or in the workplace, can have devastating and long-lasting effects on your confidence. Bullying can take the form of being undermined in front of others, singled out and treated differently, ridiculed or subjected to excessive monitoring or supervision. There are many other ways in which you can be made to feel victimized.

The moment you show that you are sensitive about, or can be hurt by something – it could be a physical imperfection, your accent, your background, your gender or your age – you become a target for a bully. You become more and more self-conscious about it, and you then mentally attack yourself because of it.

This process diminishes your self-confidence, because you perceive that people can take from you at will and you haven't developed the mental muscle to resist. You become a compulsive giver to others, before they even ask, just to spare yourself the possibility of being bullied. Giving becomes a safety measure to prevent bullying. Those who undercharge for their professional services have often been on the receiving end of bullying. They are scared to charge the going rate for their services for fear of rejection.

TOP 5 SYMPTOMS OF DOMINANCE

1 You take on the role of 'the victim' and accept the blame for everything that goes wrong.
2 You give too much of yourself to others, because you think that is what they expect of you.
3 You let other people walk all over you at great emotional cost to yourself.
4 You find it difficult to say no.
5 You find it difficult to value yourself, while attributing great importance to other people's opinions of you.

Don't allow others to walk all over you – build your mental muscle and resist them

CONFIDENCE
ECOLOGY

Just as a plant thrives in the presence of the right stimuli, such as light, nutrients and water, so confidence feeds on positive messages. Once you have learned how to combat all the negative messages that are thrown your way, you can start to focus on the positive ones instead, and these will gradually help your confidence to grow and flourish. Other people can have a significant bearing on this, however, depending on what sorts of people they are, how much influence they have over you and how they treat you.

COLD QUALITIES

Have you ever worked for someone with a cold disposition? You never felt able to take a problem to them, they criticized you whenever you made a mistake, and were cynical when you showed enthusiasm. It is very diffi-cult to feel confident in the presence of people who are critical, judgemental, cynical and dominant. Their negativity creates a very cold working atmosphere, which is simply not conducive to the growth of confidence.

cynicism

criticism

arrogance

judgement

superiority

bullying

WARM QUALITIES

On the other hand, have you noticed how confident you feel in the presence of managers who are naturally warm, encouraging and supportive? They say good things to you when you do good work, show you how to improve and help you when you are down.

encouragement

compassion

trust

belief

understanding

recognition

CASE STUDY

Tony was a talented professional footballer tipped by many critics to play the sport at international level. However, after a big-money transfer, Tony lost his form. He was still a talented player, but he had lost confidence in his ability.

It transpired that the root of Tony's problems lay in his relationship with his manager. Tony's manager had created a culture of fear at the club. Players were only ever told when they had done something wrong, and were never encouraged or acknowledged when they did something well. Some players responded to this fear culture and performed at their best, but Tony was not one of them. He thrived on warmth and support. He needed the manager to put an arm around him, to tell him what he had done well and what he needed to work on to improve. In the absence of this support, Tony's game became riddled with anxiety and he found himself dropped from the team.

Six months later, his manager left to take up the reins at another club and a new boss was appointed. The new boss was exactly what Tony needed and Tony rejoined the team. The new manager was supportive and encouraging, he believed in Tony and he gave him the responsibility of the club captaincy. As a result of this support, Tony rediscovered his love of the game and went on to win many international caps. Tony's emotional needs were being met and his confidence was able to grow.

OVERCOMING
FEAR OF FAILURE

The fear of failure can have a debilitating impact upon a person's confidence. The consequences of this fear means that we stay in our personal comfort zone. We only do what we know it is safe to do. Fear of failure prevents us from taking any risks in case we fail. Thus, when challenges and new opportunities present themselves to us, we don't meet them for fear of failing. This step of the book helps you assess your own level of fear of failure, works through the possible causes of this fear, and finally offers positive solutions to help you overcome it.

 ## TEST: ARE YOU AFRAID OF FAILURE?

To assess your current fear of failure, for each of the 10 statements below, rate yourself on a scale of 1–10 (where 1 means you agree strongly with the statement, and 10 means you disagree strongly with it).

1 I worry about what others will think of me if I fail.
2 I think of myself as a failure if I try to do something and fail.
3 I feel under pressure to succeed.
4 I would rather stay in my comfort zone and not try rather than fail.
5 I resist taking on new challenges and opportunities in case I fail.
6 I fear success in case others think I am better than they are.
7 I am afraid of success in case I have to live up to newly raised expectations.
8 My ego prevents me from taking risks in case I fail.

9 I ignore my instincts and gut feelings when they suggest I try something new.
10 I constantly think about my previous failures.

YOUR SCORE
Under 30: the fear of failure is really holding you back.
30–70: you need to work on overcoming your your fear of failure using the exercises in this book.
Over 70: fear of failure is not really having a dangerous impact on your confidence.

FEAR OF SUCCESS

As well as experiencing the fear of failure, we can also suffer from the fear of success. We don't want to succeed and stand out from the crowd, because this would mean that we have to step outside our personal comfort zone. People would suddenly notice us and we might have to live up to new expectations. People can experience fear of success because they don't want others to think any less of them, or suspect that they have become big-headed or have got ideas beyond their station. Peer-group pressure can disable a person's desire to get ahead in their life or career, simply because they are afraid of the reaction they will get if they leave their friends behind.

 CASE STUDY

The Swedish champion golfer Anika Sorensam is a great example of someone who had a fear of success.

In the early part of what was to become a hugely successful career, Anika would sometimes miss sinkable putts when she was in championship-winning positions, in order to avoid winning and thus having to make speeches, which she absolutely dreaded. It was only when she was able to come to terms with making acceptance speeches for trophies that she began to make those championship-winning putts.

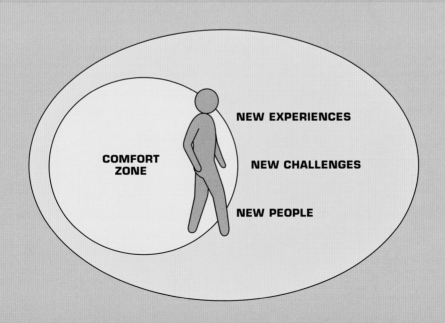

COMFORT ZONE

NEW EXPERIENCES

NEW CHALLENGES

NEW PEOPLE

FIVE MAJOR CAUSES OF
FEAR OF FAILURE

These are the most common reasons for people developing a strong fear of failure, and they are covered in turn on the following pages.

COMMON CAUSES

✖ **Over-protective parents**

✖ **Fear of the unknown**

✖ **High expectancy**

✖ **Egotism**

✖ **Previous failures**

they run out of money, they simply call their parents to ask for money to be sent to the city where they are stranded, rather than working out a solution that will resolve the problem in which they find themselves.

All of this leads the individual to the stage where they do not want to get into any situation involving an element of risk, because they automatically wait for their parents to support them before they do anything. This then has a negative impact on their self-confidence, because they are unused to handling challenges and thus back down when things do get difficult.

OVER-PROTECTIVE PARENTS

Parents who are over-protective impose strong boundaries that limit what you can and can't do. These boundaries are for the purposes of your safety, but serve to limit your ability to take risks and discover your own potential.

The over-protective parents genuinely want to help, because they can't bear to see you get hurt. They want the best for you and will do anything for you, so much so that you come to rely on them, and when the going gets tough you know that they will bail you out. A good example of this occurs when young people are travelling the world; when

FEAR OF THE UNKNOWN

Frequently, fear of failure is induced by fear of the unknown. Perhaps we are attempting to do something that we have never done before, and therefore we cannot be sure

You need to take risks to discover your potential

what the outcome of our efforts is going to be. So we stick with the safety and security of what we know, which means that no risks need to be taken and there is no chance of failure. This might mean that we ignore our instincts, which might be telling us to take a particular course of action.

For example, someone might have a great idea for a new business, but is put off initiating the idea because no one else has tried it, so therefore they think hat there must be something flawed in the idea. The reality is that they might very well have been the first person to have had the idea, but they don't trust themselves enough to take it further.

A person's instincts are designed to provide them with information that will be useful for their survival and success. A confident person will listen to this quiet inner voice and try to respond to it, whereas a person who is low on confidence will be loath to trust their instincts in case they are wrong.

instinct – confidence = mistrust

 CASE STUDY

Melanie, who was 48 years old, felt trapped in her life and desperately wanted freedom. She was in a marriage of 24 years' standing, but was in love with a young man she had met while on a business trip abroad. She was deeply torn.

She had a desperate fear of making a move abroad into something new, in case it didn't work. Her heart said, 'Yes, this is the happiness that I seek.' Something else, however, said, 'No, it's too risky. What if it doesn't work? I've been 26 years in this relationship – it's steady, it's stable, it's perfectly comfortable, yet I'm unhappy.' The question for her to answer was, 'Do I stay as I am, take no risks and be unhappy and live to regret not trying, or do I do what my heart desires, trust myself that it's the right thing to do and move into the unknown?'

She opted for the latter, since she knew that if she didn't she would not be able to live with herself. Her instincts were telling her to go, but it had been so long since she last listened to her instincts that she had lost the habit of responding to them. She chose to leave her unhappy marriage and Melanie is now living very happily with the man of her dreams and has no regrets about making her decision.

HIGH EXPECTANCY

The term 'high expectancy' means the anticipation or demand of a certain, very positive result. This level of expectancy is very often prevalent in the world of business and work, where the demand for results can stifle creativity for the following reasons:

- *To meet shareholder demand.*

- *Because jobs are on the line.*

- *Because you are paid to get results.*

The pressure is on for you to perform, and you dare not fail. So you remain in the comfort zone of what you know will work in order to prevent any chance of failure. This means that you may have to stifle your instinctive urges, which may be telling you to pursue an idea that has the potential to be very successful, but you dare not in case you are somehow wrong.

BLAME CULTURE

Perhaps you fear for your job if you fail, or you fear the wrath of your boss, who may have to take the responsibility and consequences for your failure. In other words, you are working in a blame culture.

SUCCESS CULTURE

A good manager will create a workplace atmosphere that encourages the creative staff to try new ideas, without worrying about being blamed and criticized if things don't always work out. This is the hallmark of a success culture.

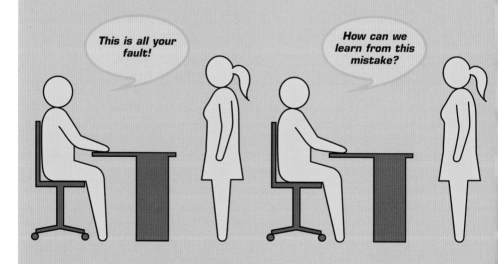

BLAME CULTURE

In a blame culture, those involved always look on the negative side of things, and fall into the following negative traps.

1 Looking to point the finger when things go wrong.
2 Indulging in politics, backbiting and gossip.
3 Hiding problems so that they fester for long periods.
4 Having a fear of initiating new, innovative ideas.
5 Dismissing the merits of what has been achieved.
6 Failing to analyse the reasons why defeat occurred, meaning that the same problems will arise again.
7 Exploiting one another's weaknesses to achieve success.
8 Failing to encourage or give praise when good things are achieved.
9 Expecting the worst in adversity.
10 Lacking self-discipline.

SUCCESS CULTURE

In contrast to the blame culture, the success culture fosters only positive thinking, manifested in the following.

1 No pointing the finger when things go wrong.
2 Providing unconditional support for each member of the team.
3 Dealing with problems in an upfront and honest manner.
4 Giving permission to try out new ideas.
5 Celebrating success.
6 Learning quickly from defeat.
7 Focusing on each person's individual strengths.
8 Each person knowing the part they play in achieving success.
9 Having no doubts in adversity.
10 Having good self-discipline and a positive attitude.

You can't have success without the possibility of failure

A STORY OF FEAR

In a village, the children were told by their parents, 'Whatever you do, don't go near the top of the mountain. It's where the monster lives.' All the previous generations of children had heeded this warning and not gone near the top of the mountain.

One day, some brave young men in the village decided that they had to go and see the monster – to see what it was really like and to defeat it. So they loaded their packs with provisions and set off up the mountain. Halfway up, they were stopped in their tracks by a huge roar and a terrible stench. Half the men ran down the mountain screaming.

The other half of the group continued on their journey. As they got further up the mountain, they noticed that the monster was smaller than they had expected – but it continued to roar and emit the stench that had all but one of the men running for their lives back down the mountain into the village.

'I am going to get the monster,' the one remaining man said to himself, and took another step forward. As he did so, the monster shrank until it was the same size as the man. As he took another step towards the monster, it shrank again. It was still hideously ugly and continued to emit the stench, but the man was so close to the monster now that he could actually pick it up and hold it in the palm of his hand. As he looked at it, he said to the monster: 'Well, then, who are you?'

In a tiny, high-pitched voice, the monster squeaked: 'My name is fear.'

EGOTISM

Sometimes people with big egos, who think that they are above average, have a strong fear of failure. The greater the personal ego, the greater the sense of loss can be should the unthinkable happen. This is a loss of status in the eyes of others, who will suddenly perceive that the egotistical person is not as powerful as they previously thought. Therefore egotists often make excuses for not doing something, so that they don't have to fail and lose face.

PREVIOUS FAILURES

If we have tried and failed before and been heavily criticized for it, this criticism and feeling of hurt can have a detrimental effect upon our subsequent attempts. We simply don't want to experience the pain again, so we don't try. Any thoughts of trying something new or experimenting with an idea are immediately linked to the pain of failed attempts.

A CONVERSATION WITH FEAR OF FAILURE

It's fairly easy to recognize when we are subject to the fear of failure. In our minds we provide ourselves with the perfect reasons why we shouldn't do something. Does this sort of self-talk sound familiar?

'I want to take a walk on a hill behind my house, but I remember how difficult it was last time, so I won't go again.'

'I'd like to learn Spanish in time for my holidays, but what if no one understands me and laughs at my feeble attempts to speak the language?'

'Maybe I should write a book, but what if the publishers reject it?'

'I think I'll apply for a new job, but what if I can't think of anything to ask the employers at the interview?'

'Maybe I should visit a friend, but what if she's not at home?'

'I'd really like to invite a girl out for a drink, but what if she says no?'

'I'd love to learn a musical instrument, but what if it's too hard?'

'I want spend a day away from the family, but what if they think I'm being selfish?'

STEP 3 Overcoming fear of failure

31

CONQUERING
FEAR OF FAILURE

Did you stand up and walk the first time that you tried? Did you form perfectly constructed sentences the first time that you tried to speak? Did you sing in harmony the first time you tried to sing? Did you balance perfectly the first time you tried to ride a bike? Were you able to swim the length of the pool the first time you tried to swim? Children learn quickly because they are not afraid to fail. Imagine the absurdity of a child who falls after they take their first step and says: 'I give up. I'm a failure at walking!'

The pressure to get things right first time inhibits the ability to learn. If you put yourself under pressure to be perfect, ease off and stop trying to aspire to mastership in a discipline that you are still learning.

SUCCESSFUL PEOPLE WHO OVERCAME FAILURE

Sir Edmund Hillary

Sir Edmund Hillary failed on his first attempt to conquer Mount Everest, but he refused to give up. After his first unsuccessful attempt, he famously said, 'Mount Everest, you have defeated me once and you might defeat me again. But I'm coming back again and again, and I'm going to win because you've grown all that you are going to grow and I'm still growing.' On 29 May 1953, with Tenzing Norgay, he successfully set foot on the highest point on Earth and became the first mountaineer to conquer the legendary Mount Everest.

Joan Jett

In 1980, Joan Jett sent a demonstration tape to all the major and minor record companies. Despite receiving a mailbox full of rejection letters, she believed in herself and her song so strongly that she finally found a record company who shared her belief. Joan Jett and the Blackhearts' classic 1980's anthem, 'I Love Rock 'n' Roll', is now estimated to be worth a cool $20 million.

Sir Winston Churchill

Churchill failed in his first two attempts to gain admittance to army school. He was tutored for the entry exam and passed – barely – on his third attempt. His father was not impressed by his

If at first you don't succeed, try, try again

son's average marks and wrote a scathing letter predicting Churchill's future to be that of a 'wastrel' leading a futile life. However, Winston Churchill went on to become British Prime Minister and, in further testimony to his strong will, he overcame a severe speech impediment to become one of the most powerful orators in world history.

Rudyard Kipling

As a young man, Kipling was fired from his job as a reporter on a San Francisco newspaper and was told by the editor, 'You just don't know how to use the English language. This isn't a kindergarten for amateur writers.' Kipling went on to prove his editor wrong, writing over 300 short stories and several novels, including the children's classics *The Jungle Book* and the *Just So Stories*.

If these people had given in at the first set-back they would never have achieved such phenomenal success

Colonel Sanders

In 1939, Harland D. Sanders perfected a secret blend of 11 herbs and spices for his 'Southern Fried Chicken'. The locals loved his original cooking, but, just as business was booming, the State built a new super highway that bypassed his restaurant. So the entrepreneurial Sanders loaded up his car with a battered cooker and drove to hundreds of restaurants looking for one that would buy his special recipe.

He faced hundreds of rejections, but with each 'No,' he was a restaurant closer to the one that would say 'Yes.' Sanders, later known as the Colonel, was rejected 1,009 times before he found anyone who would put his recipe for fried chicken on the menu in their restaurant.

INTERPRETING
FAILURE

Failure is only a problem if you interpret it as such. There may be an extremely good reason to explain why you failed in any particular situation. This may or may not have been within your control. If it wasn't, why worry? If it was, however, use the experience you have gained in a positive way to improve yourself.

THE SELF-DOUBTING APPROACH

Self-doubters use failure as proof of their inadequacy. When a person who suffers from self-doubt 'fails', they perceive themselves to be a failure. In other words, they take the failure very personally, since it simply confirms their self-view of themselves as someone who doesn't succeed. They associate themselves with the failure rather than being able to see the failure as an opportunity to learn. Often they will give up and retreat back into their comfort zone because of their desire not to repeat the experience of failure again.

This can happen after a person has been for a job interview and been rejected. They would prefer to remain in a job they don't like rather than subject themselves to the possibility of failure again. The wise person does not take the rejection personally, and learns how to be a better interviewee next time.

Self-doubters use blame and excuses to explain the unfortunate outcome:

'I can't do it.'

'I didn't work hard enough.'

'It was too hard for me.'

'It was someone else's fault.'

'I had bad luck.'

THE CONFIDENT APPROACH

Confident people, on the other hand, see any failure as an opportunity to learn and improve. They never blame themselves when they fail, but look to see what went wrong, why it went wrong and how they can learn from the experience. Confident people give themselves permission to fail. If we do this, we free ourselves from the restraints and anxiety about failing.

You may take on a personal challenge and fail. The question to ask yourself is, can you handle the consequences if you do fail? Confident people do this all the time. What separates the best in their chosen professions from the rest is their ability to handle failure. They follow the dictum:

'We will not have failure – only success and new learning.'

Confident people use failure as a source of feedback:

'I learned what never to do again.'

In summary, if you fail, look for the reason and find a solution to the problem. List possible opportunities. Ask yourself 'What have I learned?' and try again.

CONFIDENCE CHECKLIST

Ask the following questions:

- *Have I really failed?*
- *What have I learned?*

Tell yourself:

- ✓ *I'll do better next time.*
- ✓ *I'll learn from my mistakes.*
- ✓ *I can do it.*

Always try to learn from your failures

OVERCOMING
BARRIERS TO SUCCESS

On any journey towards achieving your goals, it is entirely natural to expect that some difficulties or barriers will present themselves for you to overcome. If it were any other way, being successful would be far too simple.

Success is not easily gained. You may or may not be worthy of wearing the 'crown' of success. This is why challenges or difficulties occur along the way – to see how serious you are about accomplishing success. The successful person never takes their mind off the goal they are trying to achieve. They know that the time of the greatest difficulty is very often the signal that success is not far away.

So, in overcoming obstacles, successful people are driven by a goal or a sense of mission and purpose that keeps them going forward. In their darkest hour, they remind themselves of why they are pursuing that particular goal, and this reconnects them to the desire to succeed. The goal must be desirable, or the pain of failure will be stronger than the desire to succeed.

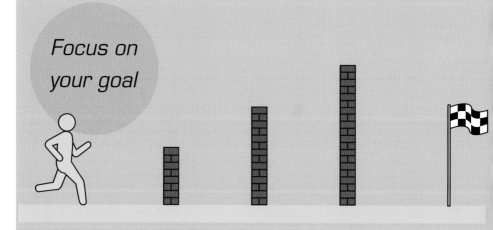

Focus on your goal

DEALING WITH FAILURE

If you have experienced previous failures, and the negative impact of these is inhibiting you from trying something new, it is important to 'resolve' your failures. When things happen that seriously affect your confidence, the imagery from those negative moments influences your behaviour.

The mind/body connection is a very powerful one. For everything that you think in your mind, your body has a reaction, regardless of whether it is real or imagined. For example, have you ever had a bad dream? Usually, you will wake up and your heart is racing and you are sweating and agitated, even though all you were doing was sleeping. In your mind, however, there was something bad going on and your body was reacting to it.

If you are alone at home, hear a noise and interpret it as the wind, you are fine; if you think it is a prowler, however, your fight-or-flight response takes over, your heart rate soars, your pupils dilate and you are scared.

Turn a negative into a positive

These are just two examples of how strong the connection is between your mind and your body. So, if you have negative imagery stored in your mind from the past, it can very easily have an adverse effect on your confidence in the present.

EXERCISE: IMAGINE SUCCEEDING

Imagine that success, or the fulfilment of a goal, is like running a 100 metre race. On the way to reaching the finishing line, you have to negotiate several problems or potential failures in the form of hurdles that get progressively higher as you go.

At 10 metres comes the first, fairly low hurdle. If you are a weak-willed person, or have very low self-esteem, you may give up at this point, saying 'Oh it's too difficult,' and not bother trying again. If you are more determined, however, you will find a way to get over the hurdle and continue the run.

When you reach the next hurdle, your attitude will again determine whether you give up or continue. So the run continues until you meet the highest hurdle just before the end. This is the big test. Will you be able to summon up the renewed strength of will and energy required to clear the hurdle and claim the prize of success?

EXERCISE: REWRITE THE ENDING

This meditative exercise is designed to help you find any negative images stored in your mind, and 'rewrite' them as positive ones.

Find a quiet place where you will not be disturbed for 20 minutes. Sit in a comfortable chair, or lie on the floor. Close your eyes, bring your focus inward and centre on your breathing. Breathe in steadily and deeply, then exhale slowly, three times altogether. Begin to relax your body, starting with your shoulders and neck, then your face, then your arms and hands, then your lower body, and finally your legs, feet and ankles.

Now imagine a path leading out from your house, and that you are walking down this path away from your house to a special place, a place where you feel safe and free, a place where you feel confident and powerful. It can be a real place or an imaginary one – a meadow, a beach, a mountaintop, a waterfall, in fact any place that is your place, somewhere you feel good. Find a place to sit down and make yourself comfortable. As you sit here, wrap yourself in a bubble of light in the colour of your choice.

Think about what happened to you. Recreate an event or story in your mind that had a negative effect upon your confidence or self-belief. Answer these questions:

• How old are you?
• What is the weather like?
• Who is around?
• What time of day is it?
• What time of year is it?
• What does it smell like?
• Who is speaking? What are they saying or doing to you?
• How does this make you feel?

Now imagine all the negative feeling caused by this event escaping out of you through a blue tube connected to your feet. Allow that negativity to run down the blue tube and out into a lake or sea that you can visualize.

Finally, rewrite the negative scene in your mind with a different outcome or ending. This is your opportunity to create the ending that you would like to have happened in that scene.

CASE STUDY

Julia had never felt comfortable singing, even though she loved music. Her insecurity about the sound of her own voice was so bad that she did not even dare sing in the comfort of her own home. She was able to trace this insecurity back to when she was young, and in particular a day when she returned home filled with excitement having had a success in the school music exam.

Julia was delighted and ran all the way home to tell the news to her parents. She got home and ran excitedly into the garden where she saw her father. She ran up to him, and told him in a delighted voice that she had got full marks in the singing exam. Instead of sharing in her delight, he looked at his daughter in a serious way and said gravely: 'I am surprised. Your voice has some faults in it, and doesn't really merit that sort of mark, I'm sure.'

His daughter was flattened by this news, and the incident made such an impression on her that it took her a very long time to overcome this lack of fatherly support. She felt very awkward about her singing, initially not wanting to sing in the presence of others, then not wanting to sing even to herself.

Thirty years later, Julia decided to rewrite this moment from her past: instead of her father ignoring her, he lifts her off the floor and swings her around excitedly, exclaiming 'Well done, my girl, well done!' He continues to show exuberance and excitement until they both collapse on the ground exhausted. Thus Julia was able to overcome her feeling of self-consciousness and awkwardness when she sang because she had successfully rewritten a moment from her negative past.

WHAT WILL HAPPEN
IF YOU FAIL?

Think about what might happen if you tried something that was outside your comfort zone and you failed. The reason for doing this is to help you recognize that the consequences of failing are never as shameful as you think they might be. If you happen to fail:

- *What would you say?*

- *What would others say?*

- *What would your boss say?*

- *What would your friends say?*

- *What would your family say?*

- *What would your work colleagues say?*

Maybe the biggest critic of failure will be you

Make a note of how you presume each of the above would react. If you believe they would be supportive, then you have nothing to fear. If you suspect that your friends, for example, would criticize you, then speak directly to them and address the matter. Ask them if they can be more supportive of you, since you want to do your best.

FRIEND   YOU   BOSS

CASE STUDY

Jake was a young tennis player who regularly criticized himself for making mistakes and not being good enough. He saw players of a similar age and capability getting ahead of him and so put himself under tremendous pressure to do better than them. Whenever he made a mistake on the court, for example, missing an easy volley, he would indulge in tirades of personal abuse. He felt that he should not be making any mistakes at all, when in reality he was still learning the game. To overcome this self-defeating habit, he took the pressure off by telling himself that he was a student of the game and did not have to be perfect. After every game he kept a log of his performance, in which he wrote down:

- aspects of his game that he did well and was proud of;
- aspects of his game that he would like to improve on, with details of how he would incorporate these into training.

By doing this, he had a clear plan he could follow to improve his game without yelling at himself for not being perfect.

WHAT WOULD YOU DO IF YOU KNEW YOU COULDN'T FAIL?

Consider what you would actually do if you were guaranteed not to fail.

What is my first step?

Write down the next step that you need to take in order to further matters.

When will I take this step?

Write down the day that you will take this step. It is important that you commit a specific time to do this, otherwise the task will be forgotten.

Who can I tell I'm going to do this?

It is important that you become accountable to someone other than yourself when you

Will you be hard on yourself if you fail?

determine to break out of your comfort zone. You will then have someone there to check on your rate of progress and to help you if you get intimidated.

HOW TO SAY NO

Many of us find it extremely difficult to say no to other people when they ask us to do something, even if doing it will cause us great inconvenience. We believe that a refusal will seem unfriendly or even hostile, and that people will not like us if we say no to them. Yet this is quite untrue – saying no in the right situation may not only alleviate stress on you but also command respect from other people. This step will help you discover how good you are at saying no, and then if necessary provide you with the ammunition you need to take a positive stand for your own good.

 TEST: CAN YOU SAY NO?

For each of the 10 statements below, rate yourself on a scale of 1–10 (where 1 means you agree strongly with the statement, and 10 means you disagree strongly with it).

1 I worry about hurting other people's feelings.
2 I say yes when I really mean no.
3 I do not dare to speak the truth to other people.
4 I want to be liked and approved of.
5 People treat me like a doormat and walk all over me.
6 I worry what other people will think of me.
7 I agree to do things because I think that is what other people expect of me.
8 I fear saying no to others in case they dislike me.
9 I have to build up my confidence before I can bring myself to say no to someone.
10 I think that people will get mad with me if I say no.

YOUR SCORE
Under 30: you need to work through this chapter thoroughly to develop the confidence to say no.
30–70: you need to continue to work on your ability to say no using the exercises in this book.
Over 70: the ability to say no is not a problem for you.

UNDERSTANDING NO

Many people have a fear of saying no to others, but **no is an influence that you can use to your advantage**. It is nothing to be afraid of. No exists to be used for the purposes of enabling a human to have choice. This is one of the features and beauties of being human. Without this choice we become like robots, with no will, and this is not the nature of the human design or purpose. No is a valuable tool that enables us to exercise this choice.

This power exists so that we do not become subject to influences that will take us away from our natural course of development and growth. However, we have to win this power, as part of our development, as part of the struggle to exercise our choice about what we will have and won't have.

Learning to say no is a natural part of development

People who say no are perceived as being cold. This is because the nature of the no influence is cold. No anaesthetizes things. It is like a cold shaft of power that prevents things from growing. No is a vital ally.

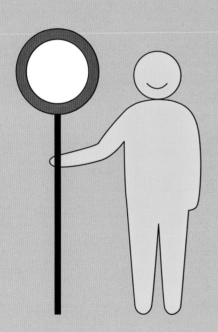

Use 'no' to stop things that you don't want

WHY IS IT DIFFICULT
TO SAY NO?

If you find it difficult to say no, you are not alone. It is probably the most common reason behind the fact that many people have difficulty in rebuilding their confidence. Those who find it hard to say no often do because they don't want to hurt other people's feelings. They worry that if they say no the other person will take offence and a friendship will be lost. There are several reasons why this might happen.

BEING PERCEIVED AS COLD

If you are a warm-hearted, generous and giving person, you will probably worry that others will perceive you as being cold if you say no. Warm-hearted people can find it difficult to say no simply because to be able to say no effectively means that you have to become a little bit cool. The quality of no by nature is a cold influence, because the function of an effective no is to be able to neutralize those things that you personally do not want to process.

PLAYING THE VICTIM

If you have a history of being bullied or victimized, it is possible that you will find it difficult to say no to others. The reason for this is that bullying causes you to take on the role of the victim. You become someone who accepts the blame for everything. Bullying leaves lots of wounds and scars in the victim; if these wounds have not healed, it becomes difficult to say no because of the fear of being wounded by the person you are rejecting. Your assumed role is that of the victim, so people walk all over you. You expect others to have more power than you do, or you simply don't use the power that you have at your disposal because it is not in your role to do so.

victim + bullying = low self-esteem

BEING SENSITIVE TO OTHER PEOPLE'S NEEDS

If you are sensitive and a friend asks you to do something for them that you don't want to do, your sensitivity will make you aware of your friend's need and also your own need. So you feel for both, which means that you become caught in an emotional tug-of-war between ensuring that your needs are met and trying to help your friend. It is difficult to say no when you are caught in this situation.

YEARNING FOR INCLUSION

One of the psychological anxieties that comes with the struggle to say no is the uncertainty of what will come back to us from others when we do. How will the person to whom we are saying no react?

- **Will they explode?**

- **Will they get angry?**

- **Will they make us feel bad?**

- **Will they make us feel a lesser person?**

If we are sensitive in some way, we will not want to hurt another's feelings, while at the same time we do not want to do things that are not right for us. This psychological uncertainty is born from the potential hurt and pain that may come our way from rejecting others, and if we have been hurt before this may be something that we certainly want to avoid in the future. So we end up saying yes in order to avoid this potential conflict and confrontation.

This yes means that the gate remains open for this other person to include us in their world, even if it is on their terms rather than our own. We want to be included in their world, because it represents an inclusion of sorts. As we seek security in our lives, we will often seek it from whatever source is available, even to our own detriment.

People who say no may be seen as cold

WHY DO PEOPLE FIND IT DIFFICULT TO SAY NO?

WARM-HEARTED PEOPLE	**are afraid of seeming cold**
VICTIMS	**don't believe they can say no**
SENSITIVE PEOPLE	**are worried about how others feel**

SAYING NO
ASSERTIVELY

If you wish your no to be taken seriously, the method of delivering it is very important. First of all, you need to believe it yourself, and to do this you will need to overcome all the common fallacies that usually get in the way and concentrate on your own rights instead.

DON'T THINK...

- If I refuse, others will feel hurt or angry.
- If I refuse, others won't like or love me.
- It's rude or selfish to refuse.
- If I refuse, I won't be able to make any requests of others.
- Their needs are more important than mine.

THINK...

- I have the right to say yes or no for myself.
- I have the right to set my own priorities for myself.
- I have the right to state the difficulties that others' requests of me will cause.

Don't forget that other people have the right to make requests of you, so you should not just respond aggressively when they do

EXERCISE: BE ASSERTIVE

Breathe deeply

Be firm in your vocal tone and body language

Start your answer with the word no

Keep the reply short and clear, but not abrupt

Give the real reason for refusing; don't invent excuses

Avoid 'I can't' phrases; use 'I'd prefer not' or 'I'd rather not'

Don't apologize profusely, if at all (one 'I'm sorry, but ...' will suffice)

Acknowledge the requester by name

Ask for more information if needed

Ask for more time if needed

If the other person repeats their request or persists in assuming that you will comply, calmly employ the following techniques.

Repeat your refusal

Slow down and emphasize the words you are repeating

State your reason, if you did not state it the first time

Don't search for better reasons

SAYING NO IN YOUR PERSONAL
AND PROFESSIONAL LIFE

It becomes more difficult to say no when the stakes are perceived to be higher. For example, it is not difficult to say no to someone who asks you if you want sauce on your pie, but when job security or a friendship is seen to be on the line, then you need to be mentally and emotionally stronger. Sometimes a little courage is called for in order to help you to change the dynamic of a situation.

Remember that courage can be found within you at all times, and this courage is simply waiting to be called upon. In the presence of your courage, others will afford you greater respect. Courage is a very powerful quality and serves those who decide to stand up for whatever they believe is just and right. Here are four typical scenarios in everyday life that you might find difficult.

1 *Saying no to taking on any more work*

2 *Saying no to friends*

3 *Taking defective goods back to a shop*

4 *Saying no to voluntary work*

1 SAYING NO TO TAKING ON MORE WORK

If you lack confidence in being able to say no, this area can cause a lot of problems. You may find it difficult to say no to your boss for fear of upsetting them, creating an awkward atmosphere in the workplace and losing a possible promotion. In addition, you may feel that saying no jeopardizes your long-term job security; so you end up saying yes, taking on more work and increasing the pressure on yourself. Your social and work–life balances suffer and you stop enjoying your work.

Your employer may not be happy about you not staying to do overtime, but it is totally reasonable to refuse when it is inconvenient for you. If you agree to do something you don't want to do, you will probably feel dis-satisfied with yourself. You may also feel angry and resentful at your boss. In this case, the no may come across non-verbally, in missing deadlines, being silent and sullen, thinking of other things when in the presence of the other person.

Self-denying behaviour and attitudes will probably reinforce the unwanted behaviour and demands of others and encourage them to keep making unreasonable requests of you. In some workplaces, you are seen to be slacking if you take lunch, for example, or if you choose to leave the office at the agreed hour of closing. This brings an unseen pressure which suggests that you are not a team player totally committed to the success of the organization. Of course, you may be the most efficient and effective member of the workforce and you get your job done, plus more, in the time agreed, but somehow that is never seen as enough.

Don't let your personal life suffer because you can't say no

CASE STUDY

Helen was expected to work late. No one asked her to. It was simply expected in the culture that had been created in the high-pressure PR company where she was employed. She wanted to go a black-tie function with her partner one Friday evening. She was dreading telling her boss that she would be leaving on time that day, since the firm was busy with a new account. Her boss would not like it. Yet she plucked up the courage to tell them. She said, respectfully but firmly, 'I understand you prefer me to work late, but today I will be leaving work on time because I have an engagement that means a lot to me. I trust that will be OK with you.' This statement achieves three things.

1 It shows that she understands her boss's needs.

2 It states what she will be doing.

3 It checks that this is OK with the boss.

Remember that for some managers, their jobs are their lives. Invariably, they are paid to handle greater responsibility. You are personally responsible for your work–life balances. If you take the position that you won't stay late to do extra work, then you may begin to educate your boss that working long hours is not necessarily conducive to extra efficiency.

2 SAYING NO TO FRIENDS

Saying no to your friends is made especially difficult because of the fear of losing their friendship and the worry about what they will say to others about you. Here is a story (opposite) to demonstrate the problem.

Use understanding when saying no to friends

In order for your no to be received well and not thrown back in your face, you will need to nurture the right feelings in the other person. The way to do this is to enable the other person to feel understood. In the case study opposite, Suzanne told her friend that she appreciated her situation, and often this feeling of being understood is actually more important than the outcome of the dealing.

Once the person to whom you are saying no feels that they are understood, this makes it much easier for them to receive your no. Their inner systems are warmed by being understood, and this warmth allows them to understand you. This leads to agreement, because you have understanding meeting understanding.

Saying yes to everyone else means saying no to your own priorities

The first task is to let the person know that you understand their situation. Then you can tell them no. Then ask them if all is clear as a result.

understanding + no = agreement

This should leave matters clear with nothing left over. In understanding another, try using expressions like these:

'This isn't the answer that you want to hear, but ...'

'I know you may not like this, but ...'

'I really appreciate you asking me to help, but ...'

'I understand your situation, but ...'

'I would dearly love to help, but ...'

CASE STUDY

Suzanne often took phone calls throughout the evening, in the privacy of her own home, from friends who used her as a free counsellor regarding their relationship problems. Suzanne was not a professional counsellor, but others had become used to her resolving their personal problems. Suzanne's whole evenings were often spent receiving such calls, since the more calls she took the more people presumed it was OK to call her. Often her friends did not even have the courtesy to ask if Suzanne was 'open' to this kind of conversation. They called her on the presumption that she was available to hear their problems. Suzanne was getting more and more drained, and her husband began to complain that they never spent any time together.

Suzanne took the calls because she was a generous person who did not want to let her friends down. She wanted to stop these 'free counselling' sessions, but she did not know what to say to her friends. She decided to seek professional advice. When her friends called, she was advised to take the call if she really had to, but not to let it run past five minutes in length. After a maximum of five minutes, she was instructed to end the call.

Suzanne was quite nervous about doing this, as she imagined her friends would think 'What's the matter with Suzanne?' and she was worried that she would be thought of in a negative light, particularly since calls had previously lasted up to two hours. Her fear was that she might lose her friends when she took this position, but she was advised: 'If they are your friends, they will want what is right for you. If they are not truly your friends and are simply using you for free counselling, it is better that you know this. The people who are truly your friends want the best for you. If there are those who might resent you saying no, why do they think that way?'

Suzanne took this advice, and found that she could say no and not feel guilty about it. She was very honest when saying no. Before the conversation developed, she would say: 'It's great to hear from you, and, as you know, I would love to help, but the truth is that I want to spend time with my husband. I appreciate that you have really urgent matters to get off your chest, but this isn't the best time for me. Is that OK?' This approach worked well, and Suzanne was truly relieved that at last she could create some time and space for herself and her husband.

3 TAKING DEFECTIVE GOODS BACK TO A SHOP

People who have less confidence than they would like often accept what they are given and don't want to make a fuss. They doubt their ability to change things. An example of this can be seen when a person goes to a shop and buys something that turns out to be unsuitable.

The unconfident person feels timid about returning it. They recognize that taking goods back requires more effort, so it becomes easier to let the matter drop. Unconfident people are intimidated by shop assistants and suspect that the assistant will take it personally if goods are returned. Remember, though, that you are not rejecting the person. You are making sure that you get what you paid for. If you accept damaged goods, you accept less. By returning the unwanted or faulty goods, you are making a good stand for yourself.

Many people worry about being thought of as a nuisance. Confidence in this situation comes from the fact that you won't pay good money for shoddy work; so you are being a nuisance, but you are doing so in the interests of fairness.

THE STRENGTH OF NO

A woman bought a leather jacket from a reputable shop. After only two weeks, the jacket fell apart. She took it back to the shop, but the staff said that she could not have her money back. Knowing that she was in the right, she refused to leave the shop until her money was refunded. She demanded to see the manager, who again tried to 'fob her off'. She still did not yield, and eventually the manager gave her a full refund. The strength of her no was stronger than the no of the shop.

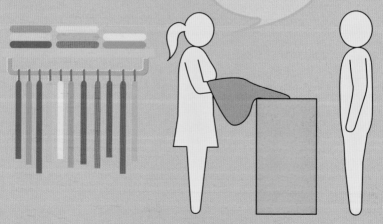

NO, I want to see the manager.

You are responsible for your own work–life balance

4 SAYING NO TO VOLUNTARY WORK

Have you ever found yourself dealing with a person who would like you to volunteer for something when you do not actually want to? You find yourself agreeing, and later you kick yourself for doing so. This is probably not the first time this has happened either. Saying no to others who ask for your help, information or resources is often difficult. Saying no may conflict with your genuine desire to help and be seen as a team player.

You may worry that a refusal will make you sound unfriendly; however, saying no is one of the things you must do to honour your prior commitments and manage your time well. Keep in mind that saying yes to everyone else results in saying no to your own priorities. No is not synonymous with being rude, unfriendly or nasty. It simply means that at this time you will not be able to accommodate the request.

Evaluate the situation

Resist the tendency to agree automatically; give yourself time to evaluate your energy and ability to accommodate a particular request and decide whether you truly want to be involved. This applies to situations that are truly voluntary, and not to job assignments couched as requests.

Explore your motives in continually saying yes. Do you have a strong need to feel useful? Many people encourage others to ask for their help. Being constantly called upon is a real boost to the ego. The down side is that your desire to be needed can be taken advantage of by others who know that they can always count on you.

Give a positive refusal

Be polite, and be understanding, but say no. Help others find other ways to solve their problems. Search for a way to be useful without doing the entire project. Offer referrals or suggestions about handling the situation. Encourage them to come to you if there are problems for which there are no other solutions, but also encourage self-reliance.

MAKING RULES
FOR SAYING NO

All nightclubs have bouncers on the door – strong, fit, aggressive people who have the power to decide who can and who can't enter the club. For example, some clubs have a 'no jeans' rule. If anyone wearing jeans tries to get in, the bouncers stop them. Other club bouncers may say 'no trainers' or 'nobody under 30'. This is to give the club distinction, or to attract a particular crowd. Without such rules, the club becomes general. Anybody can go in.

It is the same for you. If you have no rules, people can walk all over you. When you have rules, people know exactly where they stand, and they can be educated in what to ask and what not to ask. Thus you take on the role of the educator. This allows you to change the way people react to you. When you take clear, strong positions about the things you value, the radiation from this position will be stronger than the desire of the person to crit-icize you, judge you or put you down. In this way, you can change the balance of power. Give people a chance to change how they react to you. When they meet your security about yourself, they will also feel secure.

With rules you become a stronger person. You will be much clearer about what you are saying no to, and why you are saying no because you are the defender of the things you value.

*Decide
what you want
and say no to
the rest*

EXERCISE: EMPLOY THE CONFIDENCE 'BOUNCERS'

This exercise helps you put in place a strategy that will enable you to say no with greater confidence, and to understand why you are saying no. Imagine you have just bought a nightclub that represents your confidence.

The first thing to do is give it a name, such as:

THE HAPPINESS CLUB or CLUB CONFIDENCE.

Then think about the different rooms that you would like to have in your confidence club. All these rooms should reflect some of the qualities of the owner, for example:

THE CHAMPIONS' ROOM –
   where the best in other people is celebrated.

THE PARTY ROOM –
   with non-stop music and dancing.

THE DWELLING ROOM –
   a place of quiet and contemplation.

THE INSPIRATION ROOM –
   where people go in order to think original thoughts.

Lastly, and most importantly, create the rules of the club. Which instructions will you give to your confidence 'bouncers'? Which 'undesirables' do you want to prevent from entering the club? These could be self-doubt, unfortunate comparison with others, putting yourself down, or fear of speaking the truth.

Then, when you hear a little voice inside you saying:

'I'll never succeed as a ...'
'I'm not as good as ...'
'I can't tell them what I want to say'
'I dare not ...'

it is the time for the confidence bouncers to get to work. They will tell the little voice:

'I'm sorry, self-doubt/comparison/ fear, you are not a member of this club. You are refused entry.'

BUILD YOUR
NO-MUSCLE

If you have trouble saying no, the best way to gain confidence is to build up your 'no-muscle'. You can do this by practising saying no in situations that do not have a lot of emotional charge to them. Once you become comfortable, build up to saying no to the things that have more emotional impact. You will become more confident and self-assertive as you practise.

THE 'NO' MANTRA

Try to commit this little saying to memory. The more you say it to yourself the stronger your no-power will become.

When I say no I mean no.
No means no.

EXERCISE: DEVELOP NO-POWER

To help build up your no-muscle, over a period of one month make a mark (such as a blue circle) on your middle finger to remind you to practise saying no. In addition, every time you say no make a small mark or signal to yourself, such as tapping yourself on the knee three times, or stroking your nose. Then say quietly to yourself: 'I like saying no. I want to say no again.' These will become your no-power signal and phrase. When you do this for about six months, your no-muscle will develop extra power, and you will get no-power simply from making your no-signal. This works by creating

an 'anchor' for the essence of no. So through the repetitive act of making the same signal to yourself every time you say no, the signal will start to have an internal connection for you to the power of no. The following are simple examples of how you could start to build up your no-muscle.

- Don't answer the phone if doing so would interrupt your work.

- Delete all e-mails that you know are not of any value.

- Say no firmly to the telemarketer who interrupts your evening meal.

BUILD YOUR
MENTAL POWER

One of the common problems with saying no is that we have to say it out loud – but what about the art of saying no mentally? This is where it is possible to access plenty of no-power.

MAKE A DECISION

This kind of no begins with a decision – you decide that you are not going to have something, or are not going to be subject to something that you no longer want in your life. Without this initial decision, your no has nothing to gravitate around. A decision about which you are clear in your mind acts like a pathfinder: it removes the fog and shifts the doubt about which direction you should go. Habits and patterns can get ingrained in the system and can be difficult to change. A clear decision makes this change possible, creating definite leadership for yes and no to follow. Decisions come from knowing what you want (see the exercise on page 55).

PICTURE IT

Once you have decided what you don't want, imagine yourself rejecting it. Do this before you go to sleep, then first thing in the morning. These are the best times to programme. your system. To do this, consider a situation that you might find yourself in the next day –

perhaps facing the tyrranical boss, or getting involved in unpleasant gossip with friends. While picturing this scenario, imagine that you are in this situation, saying no, maybe to a demand from your boss to work late or to gossiping with your friends, even though you feel uncomfortable doing so. This no you are saying is happening in your mind. You are deciding mentally: 'No, I won't have that.' Do this before sleep and again when you wake up. Imagine the scenario that you will be facing and mentally see yourself saying no.

MAKE IT REAL

You will arrive at work or meet your friends the next day having already prepared the ground by living through the situation in your mind. This makes it easier for you to act it out physically. When the situation arises that you don't want, it will be simple to say no because you have prepared yourself mentally You have accessed the no-power that you need in your preparation. To say no, you need to have the mental no-power first.

OVERCOMING
SELF-SABOTAGE

Many people possess the ability to 'shoot themselves in the foot', often when they are on the verge of success or when something good is about to happen in their life. This step explains what self-sabotage is and where it comes from, and gives you a five-stage plan in how to counteract it effectively. This plan includes developing neutralizers, receiving confidence messages, learning to complete things, becoming a success magnet and developing willpower.

 TEST: ARE YOU PRONE TO SELF-SABOTAGE?

For each of the 10 statements below, rate yourself on a scale of 1–10 (where 1 means you agree strongly with the statement, and 10 means you disagree strongly with it).

1 Success isn't for me, it's for someone else.

2 I worry that others will be jealous of me if I succeed.

3 Everyone else is right when they blame me.

4 I usually stop just 10 per cent this side of success.

5 When I receive positive messages about myself, I think 'You can't be talking about me.'

6 I start projects and I don't finish them.

7 I am addicted to struggle.

8 I do things that destroy the relationships with the people that I love.

9 I expect something to go wrong when things are going well.

10 I do things that jeopardize my job and financial stability.

YOUR SCORE

Under 30: self-sabotage is seriously affecting your ability to succeed.

30–70: you need to work on overcoming self-sabotage using the exercises in this book.

Over 70: you are not letting self-sabotage bring you down.

WHAT IS SELF-SABOTAGE?

Self-sabotage is caused by incidents in your life that affect the way you think about success, so much so that you develop an identity, or persona, as someone who does not succeed. This means that whenever you have opportunities to succeed, in your personal or professional life, you find yourself sabotaging the opportunity. Often this is not deliberate – you simply cannot help yourself. Self-sabotage is not something that you do consciously. It is a power or influence that resides in your subconscious self and results from the combustible mix of success and failure 'exploding' inside you.

Sometimes people will self-sabotage to confirm their self-image as someone who does not succeed, which may have been created by incidents in their past. This is how they choose to be seen at a subconscious level. People can become very comfortable with not succeeding. It confirms their view of themselves that success is for someone else and not for them.

How did this self-view get there? Self-sabotage can build up from a whole range of experiences and disappointments. Here are some examples:

I'M NO GOOD AT MY JOB

- *Being stood up on an important date.*

- *Being regularly passed over for promotion at work by others less talented than you.*

- *Being mocked and put down by others, thereby constantly being given negative messages.*

- *Making a mistake that has a negative impact on your team, company or circle of friends.*

SELF-SABOTEURS

1 They are addicted to struggle.
2 They don't ever finish what they have started.
3 They put themselves down at every opportunity.
4 They exaggerate the truth.
5 They put up with negative messages about themselves.

NON SELF-SABOTEURS

1 They usually complete what they set out to do.
2 They don't punish themselves if they don't succeed.
3 They learn from their mistakes.
4 They under-promise and then over-deliver.
5 They celebrate success.

SELF-PROGRAMMING

You have been invited out on a date. You begin to look forward to it keenly, because you have been invited by someone you find really attractive. So you make sure you are looking your best. You put on your favourite outfit and arrive at the venue in good time. You then begin to wait for your date.

The appointed hour arrives and there is no sign of the date. Maybe 20 minutes pass, and there is still no sign. After an hour of waiting, you realize that the person is not going to come, so you make your way back home.

At this point you are very likely to be experiencing disappointment. This means that you have invested energy in the date. You have prepared, anticipated and waited. You have built, within yourself, 'hot-date energy'. Now, when your date does not show up, all that energy that you built in yourself for the date simply becomes unused. So, instead of you returning home happy and fulfilled that the date has worked out, with the energy all used up, you return home with the unused energy.

This is where potential trouble begins. If you return home and think to yourself 'They didn't show up because I am not attractive', you begin to programme yourself with the self-view that you are not attractive. Because this self-programming takes place at a time when you are most hurt and disappointed, it becomes more powerful. So the next time you are invited out on a date you turn it down because you can't stand the thought of being stood up and disappointed again – you make sure that does not happen by rejecting the date. This is self-sabotaging behaviour in action.

OPPORTUNITY	DISAPPOINTMENT	FEAR OF DISAPPOINTMENT	REJECT FUTURE OPPORTUNITES

Here are some common examples of ways you could self-sabotage your happiness:

Relationships
You finally attract someone who is right for you, but you somehow make it go wrong. You don't believe you deserve the right person.

Financial
You finally make some money, but then you go and make an investment that you know is unwise. You don't believe that you deserve to have that money.

Well-being
You lose your partner or job, so you go on a heavy drinking binge, even though you know it is harmful. You don't believe that you are a person of standing.

FIVE STAGES
TO OVERCOMING
SELF-SABOTAGE

The good news is that you can beat self-sabotage by working through five stages, which are described in detail over the following pages.

STAGE 1: DEVELOP NEUTRALIZERS

STAGE 2: RECEIVE CONFIDENCE MESSAGES

STAGE 3: LEARN TO COMPLETE THINGS

STAGE 4: BECOME A SUCCESS MAGNET

STAGE 5: DEVELOP WILLPOWER

STAGE 1

DEVELOP NEUTRALIZERS

To prevent self-sabotage being able to take hold whenever a negative outcome occurs in our personal and professional lives, we have to be able to develop 'neutralizers'. Neutralizers are mindsets that enable negative experiences to be effectively defused.

For example, in the case of a date not turning up, you could react in four different ways.

1 *You tell yourself 'Well, it wasn't meant to be.'*
2 *You go to a bar and pick up someone else.*
3 *You acknowledge how miserable, annoyed and let down you feel, and move on.*
4 *You tell yourself that you are unattractive, and that you can't blame someone for standing you up for that reason.*

The last approach is perfect for creating a self-sabotage mindset. You have taken the blame for what went wrong. The first three approaches, however, can all act as neutralizers. Number 1 takes a philosophical approach to the situation and attaches no blame to you for what happened. Number 2 is the most pro-active approach, and means that you can return home having had a date; the 'hot-date energy' has been used, leaving no sense of regret or remorse. Number 3 is recommended, because if you give expression to your feelings they are less likely to fester and simmer in quiet resentment.

Be philosophical

Take control of the situation

Express your feelings and move on

STAGE 2

RECEIVE CONFIDENCE MESSAGES

The messages we receive about ourselves, both from ourselves and from others, can have a major impact on our confidence. As described in Step 2, constantly receiving negative messages can be highly detrimental to the confidence-building process. By the same token, receiving positive messages can have a significant effect on building and sustaining confidence.

 CASE STUDY

Seven-times Wimbledon champion 'Pistol' Pete Sampras knows the benefit of the positive motivational message. During a difficult period in his career, Sampras often carried with him on to the court a letter from his wife, to help him through testing moments of self-doubt and uncertainty. The letter was supportive and reminded Sampras that he was a multiple champion and that he was possibly the best player ever to pick up a tennis racket.

YOUR MESSAGE

What is the message you would like to receive in moments of doubts and difficulty? Is there someone who could give you this message? Why not ask a person close to you if they would write a motivational message for you that captures the qualities and excellence that they see in you? If there is no one who can give you this message, then simply write your own.

Many people have never thought of asking someone else to provide them with such a positive message. 'Surely,' they say, 'if I want it, they will give it to me naturally?' The problem is that often the people who are closest to us don't always know what we need until we tell them. The purpose of such a message is that it reminds us of the best of ourselves at times when we face doubt and difficulty. A motivational message carries the emotional support we need to help us through the difficult times. It gives us the strength to keep going and reach our goals.

STAGE 3

LEARN TO COMPLETE THINGS

Self-saboteurs are notorious for not being able to complete things. They get bored easily and stop short of success, rather than having the discipline to see things through to the end. This means that there are many loose ends, or incompletions, in their lives that need tidying up if they are to overcome the self-sabotage habit.

WHAT ARE INCOMPLETIONS?

Incompletions are those things in your personal and professional life that you have simply left unfinished because you became distracted or bored, or forgot about them. The impact of incompletions on confidence are that they build the internal pattern of never finishing things, which means that you tend to give up before the finishing line.

If you set yourself a goal or challenge that seems inviting when you set it, the chances are that, if you are a person who never completes things or sees them through, you will move on to another goal before this one has been completed.

Things that fall into this category include:

- *A dent on your car that you have been meaning to get fixed for the last six months.*
- *A work qualification that you have stopped short of completing.*
- *A piece of artwork that you started, but is now sitting untouched in the garage.*
- *A Spanish class you enrolled for, but stopped attending after four weeks.*
- *A gym membership you took out, but have not used for three months.*

MAKING EXCUSES

Incompleters tend to be inspired at the beginning of a project, but that early inspiration evaporates as soon as they find reasons why the project is not such a good idea. The original inspiration gets overlaid by their habits and established patterns. So the person has a new initiative that feels bright and inspiring, but this new feeling is not strong enough to survive the pressure of the old habits, and eventually it withers. They then find themselves making excuses to avoid completing the project, such as:

- *I don't want to get the dent in the car repaired since I'm bound to get another dent sometime.*
- *There's no point in finishing the work qualification since I won't get promoted anyway.*
- *There's no point in continuing Spanish because I'll never live in Spain.*
- *There's no point going to the gym, because no one will ever fancy me.*

START TO COMPLETE

From now on, don't start another project until you have completed all outstanding ones. The purpose of this is to rebuild the trust and discipline in yourself to finish what you started. This will help to overcome self-sabotage, because you will build the muscle to cross the finishing line in what you do rather than giving up before completion. A good way of doing this is to find positive reasons to finish each task. So, in the examples given above:

- *You get the dent in your car repaired so that you feel good whenever you look at the car.*
- *You complete the work qualification because you want to give yourself the best possible chance of being promoted.*
- *You complete the Spanish programme to develop your versatility in languages and because you never know when it will come in handy.*
- *You start going to the gym again so that you will have more energy to complete more things.*

STAGE 4

BECOME A SUCCESS MAGNET

Get used to the notion that you can attract success. Why shouldn't you be successful? The key to becoming successful is to develop successful habits. Self-saboteurs tend to believe that success is for others, not themselves, and are embarrassed at the thought of success, while desperately craving it. Their self-sabotage has driven success away before, and therefore it is essential that they get back on good terms with success.

START SMALL

The key to becoming a 'success magnet' is to attract success a little bit at a time, so that you get accustomed to having success in your life. When actions match intentions, success occurs. When success occurs, more success occurs, because success attracts success. Lots of small successes lead to one big success, and hence to a state of great confidence and belief.

So your task is to reduce your goals into simple, manageable chunks that you can achieve effortlessly. Notice the weight that this takes off your shoulders, and how much more enjoyment you are having as you work steadily towards your goals. Beware of over-intending, putting too much pressure on yourself to succeed, or setting yourself impossible targets.

 CASE STUDY

In the sport of horse racing, English trainer Martin Pipe became champion National Hunt trainer for many years running, by sending his young horses to races where they were certain to win. He thus bred confidence in his horses by setting them simple, 'can't fail' challenges, so that they became accustomed to success. He gradually made the targets harder for his horses, but they had become so used to winning that when the major races came along they simply carried on winning.

SET YOURSELF SMALL GOALS

Imagine that Z is your target and you are currently standing at point A. From there, Z can seem a very long way away, and this in itself can cause inertia. The best way to handle this challenge is to set yourself a target, which you could call B, that represents a very simple and achievable next step forward. Look no further than reaching B. When you have reached B, set yourself the task of reaching C. This is a great formula for overcoming self-sabotage, because you look no further than the next simple goal, and on the way to the big final goal you gather a series of small successes.

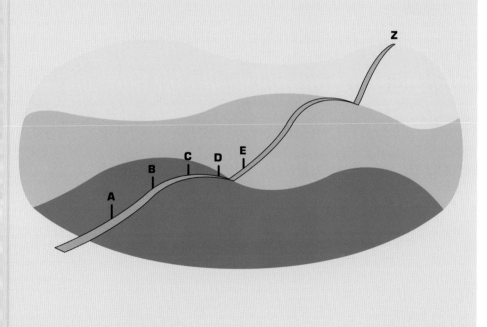

MARK YOUR SUCCESSES

Make sure you acknowledge each success that you have along the way. When you set yourself a small goal and achieve it, give yourself a pat on the back and tell yourself that you have had a success. Perhaps mark it by giving yourself a small gift or present, to confirm the success and to send yourself the message that success is good.

STAGE 5

DEVELOP WILL

One of the undoubted characteristics of those people who overcome self-sabotage is the quality of will. These people have all developed an abundance of willpower.

- *The will to keep persevering in the face of adversity.*
- *The will not to automatically accept no for an answer.*
- *The will to believe in their own capability despite what others may say or think.*
- *The will never to let go of their dream.*
- *The will to overcome odds.*

Every human being has a certain amount of willpower and everyone has the capacity to build up or strengthen their willpower. Just as lifting weights develops muscles, exercising your willpower makes it stronger.

Each time you use your willpower to accomplish something it becomes stronger. Each time you turn away from weakness and accomplish something difficult you are building up the power of your will, the power to choose your own course of action.

Willpower is cultivated in simple ways. For example, a man wakes up in the middle of the night, hears the rain falling and remembers that he has left his toolbox in the garden. He has a choice – he can forget about it, go back to sleep and collect it in the morning, or he can get up out of bed, get dressed, go to the garden, get the toolbox and return to bed.

Which action he takes will depend upon the value he has for his tools. The greater the value he has for the tools the stronger the will and desire to look after them. The question is: can he settle and go to sleep knowing that something is not right?

Willpower is the refusal to accept the limitations of a given situation and the desire to change it

EXERCISE YOUR WILL

Will is built slowly, a bit at a time. Here are some ways to develop your will:

- *Do a sponsored walk or run that enables you to go beyond your comfort zone and really surprise yourself.*
- *Read stories about people who never gave up and still succeeded, such as Helen Keller, Mahatma Gandhi or Mother Teresa. You will find that their capacity to continue in the face of adversity was forged by a strong and unbreakable will.*
- *Don't leave the dishes in the sink overnight, do all the washing up and come down to a clean kitchen in the morning. This means that you develop a habit of completing things, not putting things off, which will leave you more energized – not less.*
- *When working out in the gym, do a few extra repetitions past your targets, to develop the mental muscle of going the extra distance. The capability to do the extra reps is there within you. It's down to you whether you tap into that resource or not.*
- *If you always clean your teeth with your toothbrush in your right hand, try using your left hand instead. This will break your habitual pattern and help you develop versatility. Breaking old habits and patterns gets you better prepared for new situations.*

Give yourself the opportunity to do things you didn't know you could achieve

CASE STUDY

Mike became the manager of a football club who were experiencing difficult times. The club had developed a strong blame culture. When they conceded a goal the players' heads went down. Their body language was negative and full of self-pity. They simply expected to lose. Mike's first task was to change the negative culture. When they conceded a goal Mike taught them to see it as an opportunity to show their strength in adversity. Rather than being sorry for themselves they used the reverse to show their strength of character. By changing the players mindset, Mike was able to turn the negative culture into a positive one and the players very quickly began to achieve better results.

LEARNING TO COPE

A strong feeling of being overwhelmed by demands from work, family, social life or other sources may mean that you find it hard to cope with everyday life. This can be very hard to admit, to yourself or to other people, but admitting it is the first stage in finding a solution to the problem. This step takes you through a five-stage process: learning to cope; reducing people's expectations; overcoming procrastination; avoiding distractions; and remaining energized and relaxed.

 TEST: HOW WELL ARE YOU COPING?

To find out how well you are coping with everyday life, for each of the 10 statements below rate yourself on a scale of 1–10 (where 1 means you agree strongly with the statement, and 10 means you disagree strongly with it).

1 I don't set myself any goals because I don't want to be disappointed if I fail.

2 I can't currently see the wood for the trees.

3 I feel snowed under and can't make a decision.

4 I am never really satisfied with work that I have completed.

5 I believe that if I don't do a perfect job I am less of a person.

6 I find it hard to delegate because I don't trust others to do the job.

7 At the end of the day, I feel drained and exhausted and wonder: 'Just exactly what did I do today?'

8 However hard I work, the workload does not seem to get any less.

9 I dare not tell anyone that I can't cope, in case they think I am inefficient.

10 I take on too much in my life because I dare not say no in case others think less of me.

YOUR SCORE

Under 30: you are feeling overwhelmed and unable to cope.

30–70: you need to learn more about coping by using the exercises in this book.

Over 70: you are coping well.

FEELING OVERWHELMED

When the amount of energy that you have to give in any situation is not equal to the amount of energy being demanded, you will feel out of your depth, overwhelmed and unable to cope. This applies not just to a desk overcrowded with paper, unopened mail and so on – it could occur when making a decision, when attempting to reach a goal or target you have set for yourself, or when thinking about a deadline you are facing.

Brain 'flooding'

This occurs when we take in more information than we can effectively process. The brain loses its focus because of the volume of the incoming flood, and you consequently feel as if you are drowning. For example, you intend to spend the day working on a report, but when you get into the office your phone keeps ringing, the computer system crashes and your boss wants to see you for an important meeting, so the report gets forgotten, causing more stress. When this happens on a regular and continuous basis, your reserves of energy run out and you can't take any more demands upon you. At this point, burnout occurs, and you may need to take a holiday. In summary, the demands upon you have become greater than your ability to meet those demands.

This feeling of being completely overwhelmed has a negative effect on your confidence, because confidence comes from the simple ability to be able to do something. It is as if you simply have not got enough mental, physical and emotional resources to be able to handle the incoming traffic. What then happens is that your personal tolerances begin to become stretched.

FIVE STAGES IN LEARNING TO COPE

The feeling of being overwhelmed is like being caught in an avalanche, buried under a weight of tasks. How do you deal with it, when your energy is completely sapped by the amount that you have to do? Again, there are five stages:

STAGE 1: ADMIT THAT YOU CAN'T COPE

STAGE 2: REDUCE OTHER PEOPLE'S EXPECTATIONS

STAGE 3: OVERCOME PROCRASTINATION

STAGE 4: AVOID DISTRACTIONS

STAGE 5: REMAIN ENERGIZED AND RELAXED

ADMIT THAT YOU CAN'T COPE

Don't be ashamed of the fact that you are overwhelmed. Many people, especially those in positions of authority, consider it to be a sign of weakness to admit to others that they are experiencing this feeling of not being able to cope. It is tantamount to saying that you are not the right person for the job, because, surely, the right person for the job would be able to cope. This is not usually true – there are many perfectly logical and legitimate reasons why you might feel like this.

ADMIT IT TO YOURSELF

In the same way that an alcoholic makes the first step to overcoming the addiction by accepting that they have a drink problem, admitting to yourself that you are out of your depth is a vital first step. There may be people in your network who would be only too happy to help you cope with your current situation, but it has simply not occurred to you to ask them.

Be honest with yourself

ADMIT IT TO OTHERS

Once you have accepted the truth, you can begin to tell people you trust that you are struggling to cope. Your ego and pride may not easily allow you to do this, because to admit to not being able to cope will shatter the view that you want others to have of you as someone who is near-perfect and can handle any personal and professional situation that is thrown at them. This image-shattering may actually be a good thing, however. If you no longer have the stress of having an image to live up to, you can start to be who you really are, and not as you want others to see you.

STAGE 2

REDUCE OTHER PEOPLE'S EXPECTATIONS

If people are imposing unrealistic deadlines on you, try to renegotiate them. When you reach the point of being overwhelmed, you need to stop any new items coming into the system so that you can deal with what is already there. When you have caught up, you can then begin to reopen the systems to incoming 'traffic'.

Remember that you have both the power and permission to do whatever is necessary in order to do the best job that you can. Sometimes others don't know what your situation is, and when they do they will happily help you do a more effective job.

RELIEVE THE PRESSURE

Sometimes others have a strong attachment and draw mental and emotional energy from us when we give to them all the time. We provide power for them at our personal expense. We give, they receive, and they don't give back. We become attached to giving to them, and they expect to receive from us. They won't let us change, because they are reliant on us.

As described in Step 5, when you say no you are often helping both yourself and others. By relieving the pressure on yourself, you will find that you can cope much better with your workload, for example, and as a consequence will have more energy, strength and independence. Others will find that they are not as reliant on you as they thought, and saying no to them may even cause them to have greater respect for you.

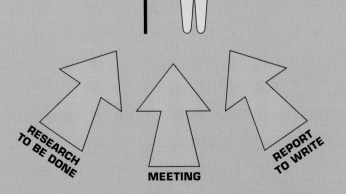

RESEARCH TO BE DONE

MEETING

REPORT TO WRITE

STAGE 3

OVERCOME PROCRASTINATION

When we experience a sense of being overwhelmed, procrastination can easily take hold. Procrastination – putting things off – includes not starting things and not finishing things. We find it hard to start either because the task we are facing seems so overwhelming we think we cannot possibly finish it, or because we have developed a highly critical picture about the form the completion will take. So we delay the completion in the hope of avoiding self-criticism.

When you become a serious procrastinator, you rehearse over and over in your mind how you are going to do something, and then, when you do nothing, it does not disturb your perfect vision. A little voice inside you says things like:

- *What if I make the wrong decision?*

- *I'd like to go to the seaside, but, there again, I'd like to stay in.*

- *I know that I really should dump him, but I keep having second thoughts.*

- *I would really like to move house, but I can't face the hassle of house-hunting.*

DEALING WITH YOUR TOLERATIONS

We all have a number of things in our lives that we are putting up with, which have a negative effect upon us, contributing to a decline in our confidence levels. These are known as tolerations or energy drains. They can range from small things such as a missing shirt button that you never get round to replacing to more important factors such as a tyrannical boss who is making life a misery for you in the workplace.

In the course of a life we will never reach a point where we have no tolerations whatsoever, but you can reduce the number of things that you are currently actively tolerating. People sometimes forget that they can take control over the things that are bothering them. When you become adept at dealing with your tolerations, you develop the self-discipline and confidence to deal with things at the time they need dealing with, whether you like dealing with them or not. This enables you to develop a 'can do' mentality.

EXERCISE: MOVE FORWARD

Make a list of five things that you are currently tolerating in each of the following situations and determine whether you can see a solution to each item or not. It does not matter whether they are big or small items. Each category has some examples to give you some ideas:

 YOUR HOME
- It is messy.
- The carpets need cleaning.
- The walls need painting.
- The furniture is old and worn.
- The attic needs clearing out.

 YOUR WORK
- I am working too many hours.
- I am undercharging for my services.
- I am in the wrong line of work.
- The future is unpredictable.
- I have had inadequate training.

 YOUR WELL-BEING
- I am overweight.
- I am drinking too much.
- I am eating a poor diet.
- I am physically unfit.
- I am smoking too heavily.

 YOUR FINANCES
- I am constantly living beyond my budget.
- I have no idea how much I spend on a monthly basis.
- I am weighed down with debt.
- I am owed money that is long overdue.
- I am being seriously underpaid.

 YOUR LIFE BALANCES
- It's all work and no play.
- I haven't had a holiday for a long time.
- I never treat myself to things I would like.
- I am taking life too seriously.
- I can't switch off.

Using the five separate lists of things you are tolerating, make a positive decision to do something about at least one item from each list. When you have achieved this first stage, move on to the next set of five tasks, and so on. Eventually, your list of tolerations will be much reduced, and you will have changed your mindset to one of getting things done rather than putting them off. This will improve your confidence, since it will prove to you that things are not always as difficult as you imagine them to be, and you will not feel so daunted by challenges – large or small – in future.

STAGE 4

AVOID DISTRACTIONS

It is important to keep your self-discipline in the face of everyday distractions. For example, it can be very tempting to absorb yourself in the internet, particularly if you are working in an office environment or are self-employed and do not have the discipline of others that will keep you focused.

Another thing that can happen when we feel overwhelmed is that we allow ourselves to become distracted as a way of not having to face the fact that we cannot cope. This makes us feel that we are doing something, which we justify to ourselves by saying 'As soon as I have just surfed the net, I'll crack on with ...'.

STAGE 5

REMAIN ENERGIZED AND RELAXED

Develop escape valves to provide an outlet for the pressure that builds up in you during periods of feeling overwhelmed, otherwise the pressure will take all of your energy. At such times, there are more demands on your energy than at most other times, so it is essential that you are fit in body and mind. Here are some good ways of keeping your energy levels up:

- *Go to the gym.*

- *Go dancing.*

- *Take energizing walks.*

- *Play sport.*

- *Have interests outside the workplace.*

- *Practise relaxation and meditation techniques.*

SOCIAL CONFIDENCE

Many of us find it difficult to talk to new people in a social situation, because we lack the confidence to chat to 'strangers' and perceive ourselves as 'shy'. Making 'small talk' is easier than you might think, and this step will show you how to develop your social skills and overcome any shyness you might have, by taking you through eight simple stages.

TEST: HOW GOOD ARE YOU AT SMALL TALK?

To assess how good you are at small talk, for each of the 10 statements below rate yourself on a scale of 1–10 (where 1 means you agree strongly with the statement, and 10 means you disagree strongly with it).

1 I dry up in social situations.
2 I forget people's names easily.
3 I find it hard to initiate conversations.
4 I find small talk superficial.
5 I worry that people will find me intrusive if I ask them questions.
6 I worry what others will think about me.
7 I feel awkward in the presence of people that I don't know.
8 I have lost my sense of curiosity about people.
9 I feel awkward about sharing my interests with others.

10 I have stopped keeping abreast of current affairs.

YOUR SCORE

Under 30: inability to make small talk is really holding you back.
30–70: you need to work on overcoming fear of small talk using the exercises in this book.
Over 70: fear of small talk is not really having a detrimental effect on your confidence.

SMALL TALK

It is called 'small talk' because it focuses on the small details of life rather than the bigger picture. It is noticeable that those people who excel at making small talk generally have a keen sense of curiosity about people and life. The ability to make good small talk comes from having an 'overspill' of references, facts and information. This means that you are filled to overflowing with references, facts and information that you want to share with others.

THE ROOTS OF SHYNESS

The inability to make effective small talk can cripple the social lives of many people. It can prevent business people 'networking' effectively. Poor social skills can prevent shy people from being able to ask someone out for a date, and can also make the workplace a misery for new members of staff who find it hard to make acquaintances. The inability to make small talk has its roots in our early social conditioning.

'Don't talk to strangers'

This warning is given to us from an early age. It is an understandable warning to a child to keep them from harm, but can become a permanent mindset, meaning that an adult does not talk to strangers because these are still regarded as people to avoid. The adult will only initiate conversations with someone they already know and trust.

'Don't pry'

Children are educated, in the interests of respect, not to pry into other people's business, because this is rude. Again, we take this attitude forward into our adult years, meaning that we dare not ask people questions in case they think we are prying into their personal lives or are being intrusive.

TOP 5 TRAITS OF PEOPLE WHO FIND SMALL TALK DIFFICULT

1 They worry about what other people will think of them.
2 They don't want to seem intrusive.
3 They feel awkward and self-conscious in the presence of people they don't know.
4 They worry about what they should say next in conversation.
5 They have lost some of their sense of curiosity about people and life.

TOP 5 TRAITS OF PEOPLE WHO FIND SMALL TALK EASY

1 They are happy to initiate conversations.
2 They have a way of making others feel at ease in uncomfortable situations.
3 They have a genuine interest in other people and their lives.
4 They are good listeners.
5 They are constantly updating their references.

'Curiosity killed the cat'

If, as children, we ask questions of our parents or teachers out of a natural curiosity to learn and discover, then, if the parent or teacher is too busy or simply does not know the answer, we are told not to ask so many questions. This educates us not to be inquisitive and to stifle our natural curiosity.

'Don't interrupt'

When, as children, in our enthusiasm to speak and make ourselves heard, we are admonished and told to not interrupt, or to speak only when we are spoken to, again this builds a mindset that makes it difficult to be spontaneous in conversation. It introduces a formal code of behaviour based on 'don't' rather than 'do', so that you end up needing permission from another person before you can speak.

All this conditioning can have a negative impact on our ability to make effective small talk as adults. When faced with people who we have never met before, these psychologies can take a firm and decisive grip, and we mentally freeze.

EIGHT STAGES TO EFFECTIVE SMALL TALK

To improve your ability to talk to new people in social situations, there are eight stages for you to work through:

STAGE 1: IMPROVE YOUR REFERENCE BASE

STAGE 2: START A CONVERSATION

STAGE 3: ASK QUESTIONS

STAGE 4: REVEAL SOMETHING OF YOURSELF

STAGE 5: DEAL WITH AWKWARD SILENCES

STAGE 6: REMEMBER NAMES

STAGE 7: MAKE AN IMPRESSION

STAGE 8: DEVELOP YOUR LISTENING SKILLS

STAGE 1

IMPROVE YOUR REFERENCE BASE

If you find small talk difficult, then set out to improve your cultural reference base. For example, try to learn and discover something new each week about any of these different areas:

- *World events*

- *Sport*

- *Trends in fashion*

- *The state of the financial markets*

- *Innovations*

- *New developments in science*

- *Business trends*

- *Recent films and books*

- *Developments in health and well-being*

- *Celebrity behaviour*

What you are looking for in order to start a conversation are points of connection. In order to be conversant, you must be well informed. In order to be well informed, you must be well read.

The more you know, the more you will have to talk about with other people

STAGE 2

START A CONVERSATION

The best way to start a conversation is with simple, non-controversial observations. You could, for example:

- **Comment on the latest news headlines.**

- **Discuss the local traffic situation.**

- **Point out peculiarities and trends in the weather.**

- **Mention the new colour scheme in the office.**

- **Talk about how your children are wearing the same fashions you once did.**

When you share your opinions and observations, other people are more inclined to do the same. When all else fails, try giving the other person a compliment.

Isn't it hot today?

Yes, I love it when it is sunny.

Don't wait for someone to approach you, start a conversation yourself

STAGE 3

ASKING QUESTIONS

Many people believe that the best way to keep a conversation going is to ask questions. Try asking someone:

- **Whether they like going to the movies or the theatre.**

- **What they thought about last night's big sports game or soap episode.**

- **Where they grew up.**

- **How long they have been in their profession.**

Ask polite questions, without being too personal

The key, however, is learning how to use questions to start a conversation, not to control it. Don't ask too many questions and avoid those that sound too probing, personal or aggressive.

Did you see the game last night?

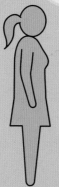

Yes, it was great.

STAGE 4

REVEAL SOMETHING OF YOURSELF

Although it is risky, when you reveal something about yourself the level of conversation can become deeper. Once you start sharing more with other people, they will start sharing more with you.

Obviously, you don't want to air your 'dirty laundry' or give people more information than they can handle. If your instinct tells you a subject is inappropriate, it probably is. Appropriate topics might be:

- **Your opinion on a recent film.**

- **Where you went to college or university.**

- **What pets you have.**

- **Your favourite sports team.**

- **Your experiences at a new restaurant.**

Reveal a few interesting things about yourself

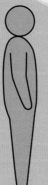

I love animals.
Do you have
any pets?

I've got a cat
called Byron.

STAGE 5

DEAL WITH AWKWARD SILENCES

One of the fears that many people have about making small talk is the awkward silence – that moment when conversation dries up and neither of you is able to find anything with which to restart the chat. The awkwardness seems to last for ever, until one of you makes a suitable excuse and the agony is over.

What can you do to prevent that occasional awkward silence when the conversation just runs out of steam? The worst time to come up with something to talk about is at the very moment when conversation has dried up, so try thinking in advance of two or three things to bring up during a lull. They could involve current events, sports or music, for example.

Think of some non-controversial topics beforehand, so that you can use them either to start a conversation or to fill in any awkward gaps

STAGE 6

REMEMBER NAMES

Many people forget the names of new people after being introduced, because either they are not listening properly or there is too much background noise for the information to be properly processed.

When you are introduced to someone, listen carefully. If it seems appropriate, you can say: 'Would you say your name again? I'm not sure I got it'; 'That's a nice name. Would you pronounce it again?' or 'How do you spell your name?' You could also repeat the person's name once or twice during the conversation; this will help you remember the name as well as letting the other person know that you know it. For example:

I look forward to seeing you again, Val.

- **Thanks, Gerald, for that information.**

- **Charlene, I really appreciate your sharing that.**

- **Helen, that was a charming story.**

- **Good to meet you, Will.**

Be careful, however, not to overdo this, since constant repetition of someone's name can be seen as a sign of over-familiarity and become irritating.

Use your listening skills to remember names

STAGE 7

MAKE AN IMPRESSION

What you say accounts for about 20 per cent of the first impression you create. The sound of your voice accounts for about 30 per cent, and 50 per cent is related to non-verbal messages, such as body language. Here are eight ways to create a good first impression.

1 PRETEND YOU ARE MEETING AN OLD FRIEND

Imagine that the person you are meeting for the first time, or are trying to impress, is an old friend you have not seen for many years. You are pleased and excited to see that person again. Adopt this attitude and the rest will come naturally.

2 MIRROR BODY LANGUAGE

When the person you are meeting folds their arms, do the same. If they lightly touch your arm, do the same to them. If you are sitting down, cross your legs in the same direction as theirs. These actions may seem obvious to you, but are rarely noticed by the other person, who will subconsciously feel that you are sympathetic towards them. When you do this, the conversation becomes more like a dance than a war.

Use positive body language to make a good first impression

3 ECHO THEIR LANGUAGE

If the person calls their newborn son their 'boy', don't call it a baby, child or infant. Call it a 'boy'. If the person refers to their work as a profession, don't call it their job. Using their special language is a form of verbal mirroring. It tells the person you are on the same wavelength.

4 LEAN FORWARD

A slight forward lean towards the person you are speaking to indicates that you are interested in what they are saying, are listening intently and don't want to miss a word of it. Leaning backward says that you are bored or uncomfortable, want to be somewhere else and are halfway there.

5 MAKE EYE CONTACT

Letting the other person know that they are the most important person in the room begins with how you think about them. Tell yourself that they are the most important person in the room. Give them your full attention, because that is how you would want others to treat you. Don't look vaguely into space, or keep looking over their shoulder to see if someone more important has just arrived. Make frequent eye contact, lasting no more than two or three seconds each time. Never stare continuously and intensely into the other person's eyes, however, since this will make them feel very uncomfortable.

6 USE TOUCH AND BODY LANGUAGE

A firm handshake on meeting someone can work wonders. To assist in developing a positive handshake, try imagining when you meet someone that you are a powerful and successful business person. The former US President Bill Clinton always radiates positive body language and one of his hallmarks is the two-arm handshake. This is accomplished by shaking the other person's right hand, while lightly grabbing their arm with your left hand. The higher up their arm you place your left hand the greater the warmth you are felt to be radiating towards them. Another of his tricks is biting his lip to indicate sympathy for another's pain or suffering. For example, if a person is telling you a hard-luck story, gently bite your lip to let them know that you feel for them.

7 VARY YOUR TONE OF VOICE

Make sure your voice is not a monotonous drone. Vary the pitch of your voice to accentuate key points. Also try to vary your speeds; a quicker speed is useful if you want to create some excitement in the conversation, and a slower speed helps if you want to create some calm and reflection. If you want to create some intimacy, speak in a quiet voice, almost a whisper.

8 INVOLVE YOUR LISTENER

Some people try to cover up their nerves by talking continuously. They fear that their audience will not find them interesting, so don't risk leaving a pause in the conversation in case people make their excuses and leave. So try to break up your conversation. Check that the listener is still with you by asking them what they think about what you are saying, or whether they have any points of view. Invite them into the conversation rather than excluding them.

Mirroring their language tells them you're on the same wavelength

STAGE 8

DEVELOP YOUR LISTENING SKILLS

If you have a poor attention or listening span, then small talk is probably hard work for you. The ability to create space for others is as important a skill in small talk as asking starter questions.

It can be difficult being quiet enough inside oneself to be able to listen. When we listen, conversation is easy. When our heads are full of wondering what to say next, then we miss the flow of the conversation, and it does not get out of first gear.

To develop your listening skills, spend one minute per day doing nothing but listening. Listen to the sounds around you.

- *How many different sounds do you hear?*

- *Which are close to you and which are far away?*

- *Are the sounds deep or shrill?*

- *Are they harsh sounds or soft sounds?*

In other words, listen properly and learn to analyse what you hear. Become a sounds connoisseur. This will lead to increased still-ness and enable you to hear the words of others much better.

PUTTING THE THEORY INTO ACTION

Remember that small talk is anything but trivial. People do business with people they know, like and trust. There is no better way for people to get to know you than by you talking to them. Although engaging a person you don't know in conversation may be difficult, don't give up on it. The art of small talk takes plenty of practice, as the eight stages above have demonstrated.

MAKING SPEECHES
AND PRESENTATIONS

Fear of public speaking – whether it be a small private presentation at school, college or work, or a full-blown formal after-dinner or wedding speech – is reported to be one of the greatest fears in adults across the world. Even those people who are normally quite confident in other areas of life can be reduced to a nervous wreck just by the thought of it. This step will help you conquer your fear and become a successful public speaker.

TEST: HOW CONFIDENT ARE YOU AT PUBLIC SPEAKING?

To assess your current state of confidence in public speaking, for each of the 10 statements below rate yourself on a scale of 1–10 (where 1 means you agree strongly with the statement, and 10 means you disagree strongly).

1 I feel anxious when I learn that I will perform in front of others.
2 I attempt to avoid giving any presentations if I can get out of doing them.
3 I suffer from a lot of anxiety about my presentations ahead of time.
4 I feel uncomfortable being in the spotlight when speaking in front of others.
5 I worry about embarrassing myself in front of others.
6 I worry that others will criticize me when I make presentations.
7 I am afraid to let others see that I feel fear and vulnerability.
8 I worry that I will dry up when I make a speech.
9 I feel that I will lose credibility if I make an ineffective speech.
10 I worry that others will ask me a question that I can't answer.

YOUR SCORE
Under 30: you really do fear public speaking.
30–70: you need to work on your public speaking skills using the exercises in this book.
Over 70: you have the confidence to speak in public.

WHY DO WE HAVE A FEAR OF PUBLIC SPEAKING?

Without doubt, this is an area that can cripple a person's confidence. The thought of having to make a speech or presentation is often greater than making the speech itself. For many under-confident speakers, the fear arises because, suddenly, you are the centre of attention. Everyone is looking at you, waiting to hear what you have to say. You feel that people will laugh if you make any mistakes or 'dry up' through sheer nerves.

In truth, however, this is probably not the case at all. Your audience, collectively, may appear daunting, but is made up of individuals who are most likely very interested in what you have to say, and will accord you the respect you deserve if you only give them a chance to do so.

TOP 5 TRAITS OF PEOPLE WHO EXCEL AT MAKING SPEECHES

1 They want to share what they know with others.
2 They enjoy building a good rapport with people.
3 They don't feel under pressure to be perfect.
4 They trust in their own ability to handle a difficult audience.
5 They always learn quickly from their mistakes.

FOUR STAGES TO SUCCESSFUL PUBLIC SPEAKING

Overcoming your fear can be tackled by working through the following stages:

STAGE 1: WIN OVER THE AUDIENCE

STAGE 2: IDENTIFY YOUR KEY MESSAGE

STAGE 3: LEARN PRESENTATION SKILLS

STAGE 4: INTERACT WITH THE AUDIENCE

WIN OVER THE AUDIENCE

The biggest single anxiety that people have when it comes to making speeches and presentations relates to the audience. What is the relationship between the speaker and the audience? Perhaps you feel self-conscious and the attention that you are suddenly receiving becomes a pressure to perform to meet the expectations of the audience. You feel that you will be judged by the audience and made to feel a fool, and that in the spotlight your personal world is suddenly open to scrutiny. Thus, the speaker in an act of self-protection becomes defensive about making the speech so that previous wounds don't get reopened.

In a one-on-one or small-group situation, a speaker can adjust what they are saying to meet the responses of the individual or group and make sure their needs are addressed. In a speech, you can't neutralize the individual quite so easily, and often this is the unspoken fear of the unconfident speaker. In an audience situation everything gets amplified; so, if one person starts to become unsettled and argumentative, you worry that this will spread like a virus to the rest of the audience.

This can produce a very great internal pressure and the performer can become highly sensitive to potential audience reaction.

- *Will they judge me?*

- *Will they criticize me?*

- *What if they don't listen?*

These questions dominate the unconfident speaker's thoughts, eat away at their confidence and make the speech or performance an exercise in personal torture.

the messenger +
the message = the mission

SHARING YOUR WISDOM

A good way to think when making a speech or presentation is that you are there to share your wisdom. Talk to one person at a time. Literally, look directly into the eyes of one listener at a time, just as you normally do in one-on-one conversation. This will be difficult at first if you are used to scanning or avoiding eye contact, but it is worth the effort to acquire this basic habit of effective speech.

CASE STUDY

Tony was a successful and famous concert pianist. The number one lesson that he had learned after 15 years in his career as a professional musician was that the role of the audience is to witness the musician's attempt to connect to and transfer the essence of music.

This means that the musician's first dedication is always to the music. Each performance provides the musician with an opportunity to build their living connection to music. Without this connection, the audience will feel nothing from the performer. When the musician connects to the essence of music, the audience can have an unforgettable experience. Thus the role of the musician is to be a messenger, and the role of the audience is to be witness to that message.

A performer who believes this is much less subject to the vagaries of the audience. Even if there only five people in the audience, the performer can still see it as another chance to connect to the thing they love to do the most and share this with others.

WHO HAS THE POWER?

A woman works in a research laboratory. She has to make presentations about her research, but lacks confidence in doing so. These presentations are for colleagues who are there to provide tips and objective criticism. This makes her very tense because she feels sensitive to this potential criticism and worries that she is going to be judged by the audience. She is sensitive to potential criticism because she takes it personally, having been hurt and wounded before by criticism.

This takes her away from her key messages and focus. She has made the fatal speaker mistake of becoming subject to the perceived power of an audience. The audience is unaware that it has such power. In her mind, the role of the audience has become magnified beyond its real power.

STAGE 2

IDENTIFY YOUR KEY MESSAGE

The next task is to be clear about the key message or messages that you want to present. Your task is to be a messenger on behalf of those key messages. This enables you to be neutral with regard to whether the audience likes you or not. It is not really about you – it is about the message. The audience either gets the message or it doesn't. Being a messenger on behalf of the message allows you to become very clear in your role.

DEVELOPING 'OVERSPILL'

When making a speech or presentation, it is important to have 'overspill' – in other words, to be overflowing with content, ideas and thoughts about your chosen subject. If you can, spend every available moment before your speech thinking about it, collecting examples, researching and talking to others. Live it and breathe it. This is the way to generate overspill. It means that you have something to give and therefore need an audience to give it to.

Be clear about your key message

STUDYING THE GREAT SPEAKERS

To develop your communication skills, why not listen to recordings of the speeches of some of the best speakers who have taken to the world's stages? The following are excellent examples.

Sir Winston Churchill
'We will fight them on the beaches' (1940)

Malcolm X
'The ballot or the bullet' (1964)

John F. Kennedy
'Ask not what your country can do for you' (1961)

Martin Luther King, Jr
'I have a dream' (1963)

Franklin D. Roosevelt
'A date which will live in infamy' (1941)

STAY RELAXED

It is important to stay relaxed when you are making a presentation, especially if you suffer from nerves. Here is a simple tip to help you settle your nerves. Take a slow, steady in-breath. Now imagine you have a tiny feather on the end of your nose and, as you exhale, do so as gently as possible, so that the feather is not dislodged. Concentrate only on the feather. This deep-breathing technique will calm you down.

Stay relaxed by breathing slowly and steadily

STAGE 3

LEARN PRESENTATION SKILLS

Delivering an effective presentation begins well before you get on stage. It begins with the preparation you have done beforehand. Here are some tips and exercises to help you improve your preparation. The following exercises will enable you to take greater control.

EXERCISE: IMPROVE YOUR MENTAL AGILITY

The purpose of this exercise is to help you develop a greater mental agility and versatility, excellent for when you may need to think on your feet. This exercise is best done with a partner.

Stand facing your partner, about a metre (3 feet) away. Ask your partner a question, such as: 'Give me four girls' names beginning with the letter C.' Your partner might reply: 'Charlotte, Clara, Cathy, Chloe.'

Your partner then asks you another similar question, such as: 'Give me the names of four countries beginning with the letter S.' You might reply:

'South Korea, Surinam, Scotland, and Sweden.'

Take turns asking each other simple questions like this. Don't make it too difficult. The aim is to develop accuracy and speed. Do this exercise at a fast pace for 10 minutes. When you have finished, you should feel mentally bright, quick and sharp.

EXERCISE: PROJECT YOUR VOICE

This exercise will help you when you are addressing a large audience.

While reading out loud, imagine that the words are like arrows shooting out of your mouth towards your intended target. Start the exercise with a target that is fairly close, and then progress to ones that are

increasingly further and further away:
• project the words 1 metre (3 feet);
• project them to the end of the room;
• project them out of the house and across the street.

EXERCISE: BALANCE THE TWO HALVES OF THE BRAIN

This exercise helps to balance the left (the logical side) and the right (the creative side) of the brain, and to get them working in harmony.

Most individuals have a preference for one of these styles of thinking; some are more 'whole-brained' and equally adept at both modes. Left-brain people focus on logic, order, structure, analysis and accuracy. Right-brained subjects focus on aesthetics, feeling and creativity.

Take two juggling balls, or other soft balls, one in each hand, and gently throw them to your partner, about a metre (3 feet) away, making sure that they land in their hands. Your partner throws them back to you. Throw the balls back and forth for at least five minutes. Don't make it difficult. Try to develop a nice gentle rhythm as you do this. When you finish this exercise, you should feel steady, cool and balanced.

EXERCISE: VARY YOUR SPEED OF DELIVERY

Practise reading at different speeds.

Take a piece of writing and try reading out loud:
• very slowly;
• very quickly;
• very steadily and methodically.

After this exercise, you will feel that you can make a presentation at your preferred speed, rather than rushing it because you are nervous or worried about the reaction of the audience.

EXERCISE: DEVELOP VERSATILITY

This exercise will help you develop versatility in your presentation skills.

Imagine that you are reading out loud to:
• a child;
• a grandparent;
• a head of state;
• an audience of 10,000.

How is your reading speed different for a child and a head of state? How is your tone of voice different when you are delivering to an audience of 10,000, as compared with when you are reading to a grandparent?

STAGE 4

INTERACT WITH THE AUDIENCE

The way in which you interact with your audience will determine how effective your presentation will be. Poor communicators often put their audience to sleep by hiding behind slides or other visual aids. These are useful for putting key information across, but too many means that you lose eye contact with your audience.

Don't be frightened to speak from the heart. If you feel passionately about your subject, let the audience feel that passion. Passion helps make a talk memorable, because it increases the rate of knowledge transfer between the speaker and audience.

If you are using a podium, remember that you can walk out from behind it. Sometimes speakers get attached to the power the

podium implies. Former US President Bill Clinton gave a good example of how to do this during the 1992 presidential debate with George Bush and Ross Perot. Clinton walked out in front of his podium and addressed individual people in the audience while his opponents stayed behind their podiums. This gave the impression that they were hiding while Clinton was being honest and open.

Share your wisdom

Talk to one person at a time

Be passionate about your subject

ANSWERING DIFFICULT QUESTIONS

Many unconfident speakers have a great deal of fear about being asked a difficult question. They fear that their limitations will be exposed, the audience will no longer take them seriously and they will lose face. The problem arises when the speaker places themselves in the role of expert – the person who has all the answers to all the questions.

This adopted role places an enormous amount of pressure on the speaker to be perfect. So how you position yourself in the eyes of the audience is vital. An ideal way to begin the talk is to let the audience know your background and expertise, and the reason why you are making this presentation. Let them know about the areas that you excel in, so that they feel confidence in who you are and what you can do. This will settle the audience. Let them know that you may not have all the answers, but that they are welcome to ask you questions. Tell them that, if they ask you a question to which you don't have an immediate answer, you will promise to get back to them within seven days. Ask them if

> *Answer questions if you can, or promise an answer within a set time limit*

this is OK. When you set up your presentation in this way, you let the audience know the rules by which you will both proceed. You have taken the pressure off yourself by not pretending to be the expert.

PUTTING THE THEORY INTO ACTION

In summary, when faced with making a speech or presentation, remember to:

- Practise your oratorical skills.
- Learn from great speakers.
- Stay relaxed by breathing slowly and steadily.
- Be clear about your key message.
- Be passionate about your subject.
- Share your wisdom.
- Talk to one person at a time.
- Interact with the audience.
- Answer questions if you can, or promise an answer within a set time limit.

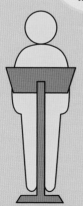

I'll get back to you on that next week.

UNFORTUNATE
COMPARISON

Our confidence levels may be lower than they ideally should be merely because we are constantly comparing ourselves unfavourably with other people who appear to be happier or more successful than we are. This step explains why we are so quick to make comparisons, and then gives advice on how to minimize this tendency by appreciating what we have got – after all, there are many other people who are in worse situations than us – and by learning to enjoy the success of others as well as our own.

 TEST: ARE YOU COMPARING YOURSELF WITH OTHERS?

To assess how much you compare yourself with others, for each of the 10 statements below rate yourself on a scale of 1–10 (where 1 means you agree strongly with the statement, and 10 means you disagree strongly with it).

1 I look at others and envy what they have got.

2 I resent others for their success.

3 I think I should have done more with my life.

4 I tell myself that I am not as good as ...

5 When I have a success, I tell myself that someone else would have done it better.

6 I think the grass is greener on the other side.

7 I forget about my own strengths and qualities.

8 I look at others and think 'I will never be where they are.'

9 I feel insecure about who others are and what they do.

10 I don't enjoy seeing others succeed.

YOUR SCORE

Under 30: unfortunate comparison is draining your confidence.

30–70: you need to work on overcoming comparison using the exercises in this book.

Over 70: unfortunate comparison is not a serious flaw.

WHAT IS UNFORTUNATE COMPARISON?

One common, yet unconscious, way in which we reduce our confidence is by comparing ourselves to others, especially to people who are further up the wealth/career/looks/ skills ladder than we are. Inevitably, our confidence plummets. Very often the person we compare ourselves with, or are jealous of, has something we want or are searching for.

For example, they may be where you want to be in your company or profession. In this instance, it's not the person that you are jealous of but the fact that they have achieved the thing you want. It may be that they have looks that you are envious of. Perhaps you are a person who always discounts yourself and think that you are not important, and that others are more important than you are.

HOW COMPARISON EVOLVES

Comparison begins with competition when we lose our first running race and realize that someone else is faster than us. It continues through school exams, when someone else gets a better grade than us. It affects us as teenagers when our boyfriend or girlfriend leaves us for someone else. It carries on into our careers when we are passed over us for a promotion in favour of someone else. It is there in our later years when we see people with less talent than us succeeding.

TOP 10 MESSAGES OF UNFORTUNATE COMPARISON

1 The neighbours are making more money than we are.
2 My sister attracts more intelligent guys than I do.
3 The boss drives a bigger, faster car than I do.
4 My brother has a bigger house than I do.
5 Other people in the gym are fitter than I am.
6 I'm not good enough to work for the best companies.
7 My friends are more attractive than I am.
8 My work colleagues are more effective presenters than I am.
9 My mates are better socializers than I am.
10 My father was more successful than I will ever be.

THE INFLUENCES
THAT CAUSE US TO COMPARE

Advertising suggests to us that there is the perfect car to drive, the perfect figure to have, the perfect house to own, the perfect lifestyle to aspire to and so on. The pressure to look just perfect is huge. In Hollywood, for example, it is no longer acceptable just to be a great actor. To succeed in the cut-throat movie business, you need either to be a superb character actor or to have stunning looks, or even both. Now men and women all over the world want to look like film, television or pop stars. When people go for cosmetic surgery today, 75 per cent of them describe a celebrity feature that captures the look they are trying to achieve.

BODY IMAGE

Do you think to yourself: 'I'm too fat. I'm too skinny. Is there something wrong with me?'

Although self-esteem applies to every aspect of how you see yourself, it is often mentioned in terms of appearance or body image. Body image is how you see yourself, and how you feel about your physical appearance. We tend to relate self-esteem to body image for several reasons.

Most people care about how other people see them. Unfortunately, many people judge others by things like the clothes they wear, the shape of their body, or the way they wear their hair. If a person feels that he or she looks different from others, then body image and self-esteem may be affected negatively.

Some people think they need to change how they look or act in order to feel good about themselves; but if you can train yourself to reprogramme the way you look at your body, you can defend yourself from negative comments – both those that come from others and those that come from you.

The first thing to do is recognize that your body is your own, no matter what shape, size or colour it comes in. Remember that it is no one's business but your own what your body is like – ultimately, you have

Would you really be happier if you looked taller or shorter, had curly hair rather than straight hair?

CASE STUDY

One of the last people you would expect to find mentioned in a study of unfortunate comparison would be the American tennis champion Andre Agassi. However, at the French Open Championships in 2001 an extraordinary thing happened to Andre. He was playing Sebastian Grosjean and was winning easily, when two games into the second set, former US President Bill Clinton arrived, to a massive ovation.

Agassi was totally thrown, as if his world had been usurped. He stopped playing his normal game and for the next two sets his opponent swept him away. Then Clinton, clearly shocked by what he was seeing, left. Agassi immediately improved. Clinton then returned and Agassi fell apart again. Agassi lost. His confidence was destroyed by the arrival of a personality greater than his own.

to be happy with yourself. Remember, too, that there are things about yourself you can't change, such as your height and shoe size, and you should accept and love these things about yourself. If, however, there are things about yourself that you do want to change, make clear goals for yourself. For example, if you want to lose weight commit yourself to exercising three to four times a week and eating nutritiously. Accomplishing the goals you set for yourself can help to improve your self-esteem.

FIVE STAGES TO BEAT UNFORTUNATE COMPARISON

There are five stages to work through:

STAGE 1: THINK ABOUT OTHERS

STAGE 2: DEVELOP APPRECIATION

STAGE 3: BE SELF-ENCOURAGING

STAGE 4: LEARN THE LANGUAGE OF CONFIDENCE

STAGE 5: BE THE VERY BEST YOU CAN BE

STAGE 1

THINK ABOUT OTHERS

It is so easy to be jealous of someone else's success. Jealousy is a very draining quality to have and it has a negative impact on confidence, because it leads to the view that others are better than you and that what you do is not significant.

Sometimes, supposedly 'superior' rivals or colleagues derive energy from knowing that others are looking at them and thinking, 'You are so much better than I am.' Try to resist feeding their egos in this way. The message you are sending to yourself is, 'I can't achieve what they have achieved.'

There is another view, however, that you can have of someone who appears to be more successful than you are. Why not use their success to inspire you rather than to drag you down? For example, you could try asking yourself:

• *What can I learn from them?*

• *What is it about them that I am jealous of?*

• *What is it they are doing that, if I did it, would enable me to reach their level of success?'*

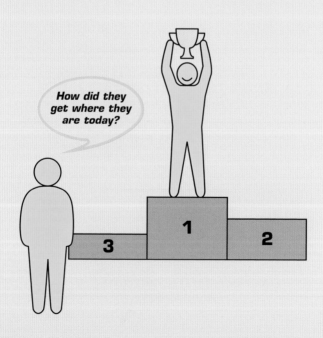

How did they get where they are today?

STAGE 2

DEVELOP APPRECIATION

When people suffer from unfortunate comparison with others, they often overlook the good things that they have in their own lives. It is an excellent idea to take stock of your own life from time to time, as a reminder of all the positive things that you have, rather than just worrying about what you don't have.

Many of us fail to notice the little things that make life so sweet. In a culture that promotes the idea that 'bigger is better', it is easy to forget to take time to appreciate the simple joys, the little gifts that life gives to us each day. Simple joys are around us at every moment – all we need is to be aware of them.

GRATITUDE MOMENTS

Try to make some time in your life for moments for gratitude. These are moments when you can express simple appreciation for the good things in your life. For example:

- *I appreciate my supportive and loving family.*

- *I appreciate my work and the people I work with.*

TOP 5 TRAITS *OF PEOPLE WHO COMPARE THEMSELVES WITH OTHERS*

1 They think the grass is greener on the other side.
2 They forget about their own strengths and positive qualities.
3 They look at others and think, 'I will never be where they are.'
4 They are jealous of other people's success.
5 They use others as ideals.

TOP 5 TRAITS *OF PEOPLE WHO DON'T COMPARE THEMSELVES WITH OTHERS*

1 They feel secure about who they are and what they do.
2 They learn from the best of others.
3 They see others as partners, not competitors.
4 They enjoy seeing others succeed.
5 They have an intimate sense of personal trust about who they are and what they do.

STAGE 3

BE SELF-ENCOURAGING

Another way that insecurity can lead to comparison is when we don't get confirmation and encouragement from others after we do good work. If this happens on a regular basis, it creates a feeling of uncertainty that can be alleviated by self-confirmation. The following exercise gives an example of how self-confirmation works.

 EXERCISE: SELF CONFIRMATION

If you are always comparing yourself unfavourably with others at work, try practising this exercise in self-confirmation.

Make a list of the qualities that you bring to the workplace and remind yourself of them before you begin work each day. Rather than thinking too much about how good others are, what about how good you are?

WHAT AM I GOOD AT?

✓ *I'm patient.*

✓ *I'm well organized.*

✓ *I'm really good at listening to people.*

✓ *I'm good at solving difficult problems.*

STAGE 4

LEARN THE LANGUAGE OF CONFIDENCE

Fragile confidence can be very easily undermined by the way in which we speak to ourselves. We may do something slightly wrong and call ourselves 'stupid'. We drop something and we accuse ourselves of being 'clumsy'. Most people carry on an internal silent conversation with themselves during much of the day. This 'self-talk' has a direct effect on our thoughts and behaviour.

Research shows that approximately 87 per cent of the things we say to ourselves about ourselves are negative, self-destructive and undermining. You have probably heard the term 'self-fulfilling prophecy'. Self-talk is very much like a self-fulfilling prophecy – something you think about so much you can actually make it happen. When your self-talk is positive ('things will work out,' 'I know I can do the job'), you are giving yourself permission to succeed and so you probably will. When your self-talk is negative ('I know I'll have a terrible time,' 'I'm not good enough to be a manager'), you are giving up on yourself, and therefore you will probably not even try to succeed. Often your internal self-talk reflects the values and behaviour you learned as a child, and the self-esteem that you now have as an adult.

THOUGHTS AND BEHAVIOURS

Self-talk can direct your thoughts and behaviour. If you think, 'I know I can do the job,' you will be more willing to apply for it. During the interview, you will be more likely to show confidence in yourself and your abilities, and have a better chance at success. If you say to yourself 'I'll never get hired for the position,' you may not even apply for it, guaranteeing that you will not get the job.

PHYSICAL AND MENTAL EFFECTS

Negative self-talk can increase your distress and can make effects such as headaches or stomach pain much worse. It can also encourage you to behave in self-destructive ways, further distressing your body ('No one cares, so why shouldn't I have another drink?'). Fortunately, positive self-talk can have the opposite effect, leading to a confident, positive attitude.

87% NEGATIVE SELF-TALK

13% POSITIVE SELF-TALK

NEW SELF-TALK

For example, imagine that a new, difficult assignment is given to you at work. You could think, 'I can't do this. It's too difficult. I don't know how to do this job.' However, why not talk to yourself differently about the task? For example, you could say to yourself, 'Look at the challenge. This task, regardless of how difficult it may seem, gives me an opportunity to learn new skills.' Below are some examples of negative and positive forms of self-talk.

USING POWER WORDS

Positive affirmations have been utilized by the self-development industry for a long time, as a surefire way of programming your mind to help you attract to yourself the things that you want. For example, if you wanted to pursue wealth, the affirmation might be: 'I am wealthy.' The problem with this is that, if you are not wealthy, the subconscious mind can easily dismiss the suggestion, as it is not your current reality. It is rather like affirming that you are 2 metres tall, when you are in fact 1.85 metres. When you use the words 'I am' to yourself, then you open yourself up to dismissal from the subconscious.

A more effective way to programme yourself is with the use of power words. Say, for example, that you wish to acquire wealth. You may have been using the affirmation:

PROBLEM	NEGATIVE MESSAGE	POSITIVE MESSAGE
Rejection	'What if they say no?'	'What if they say yes?'
Comparison	'I'm not as good as ...'	'What can I learn from ...?'
Obstacles	'It's a problem.'	'There is a way around this.'
Perfectionism	'I did OK but ...'	'I'm satisfied that I did my best.'
Others	'What will others think of me if I do that?	'I'm my own person.'
Results	'What if I make a mistake?'	'I wonder what the experience will be like?'
Age	'I'm too old to do that.'	'I may be in my later years, but I'd love to try.'
Defeatism	'I can't do it.'	'I don't have to do it perfectly.'

*If I had
£1 million what
would I do?*

Where would I live?

What car would I drive?

*To what cause would
I donate part of
my wealth?*

'I am wealthy.' When using power words, however, the word to use is 'wealth'. In quiet consideration, think about the different concepts of wealth and what it means to you. What kind of lifestyle changes would you have to make to attract wealth?

By thinking about the concept of wealth, you are instructing your conscious mind to tell your subconscious mind to personalize what the word means to you. You create in your subconscious your reality of the word. You leave no doubt as to what the word encompasses, without having to try to fool your subconscious mind into believing that you already have it.

Practise the concept of power words on a regular basis. Choose a new word each week and during your quiet time, contemplate what the word means to you. Here are some different positive examples:

- *Wealth*
- *Inspiration*
- *Health*
- *Energy*
- *Wisdom*
- *Intelligence*
- *Strength*
- *Belief*

STAGE 5

BE THE VERY BEST YOU CAN BE

Whenever we undermine our confidence by comparing ourselves unfortunately with others, we also undermine our own sense of uniqueness. Of course, we may not be perfect at what we do, but the reality is that we are not meant to be. Of course, there are others who can do what we do better, but there are also others who are not as good as we are.

From those who are better than us, what can we learn? For those who are not as accomplished as we are, what can we teach them? Understanding one's place and purpose in the world has occupied the minds of some of the world's greatest thinkers over the ages. So what is the true position where you, yourself are concerned?

When confidence is low, it becomes easy to be self-discounting, or to have the view that who you are and what you do does not matter. Confident people see that what they do does matter, and they always attach significance and importance to their activities. For example, a schoolteacher who teaches their class with care and respect is significant in the lives of their pupils. Thus, this schoolteacher is the best schoolteacher that they can be. A sales professional who works to ensure that their clients receive the best

REASONS FOR HAVING A PERSONAL MISSION STATEMENT

- **A clear and concise mission statement gives you a compass to guide you through life.**
- **A mission statement acts as a lantern, an anchor or at times a conscience.**
- **It should reflect your core values. It is like your personal constitution, the supreme law from which you make all your decisions.**
- **It enables you to represent and reflect the deepest and best from within you.**
- **A mission statement is drawn out from the quality of your inner life and has a deep connection to your values. (For example, Harley Davidson's values are: 'Tell the truth; be fair; keep your promises; respect the individual; encourage intellectual curiosity.')**
- **A good mission statement is there to inspire and propel you.**

possible customer service is significant in the lives of their clients. Thus, this sales professional is the best sales professional that they can be. The trend in these examples is that the individual is endeavouring to be the very best they can be at whatever they have chosen to do. They all have a significant part to play in the world. The schoolteacher and the sales professional are only two of the very many roles that it is possible to play. Each role constitutes a small picture in the stained-glass window of life.

To make this significance conscious, it helps to have a personal mission statement. Mission statements have got a bad name in business, simply because they tend to be very wordy and are created by consensus. A good mission statement, however, can be invaluable in providing a sense of focus, direction and purpose to your life.

CREATING YOUR PERSONAL MISSION STATEMENT

Begin this process by brainstorming. Write down everything that is important to you. Think about all the different aspects of your life: family, career, friends, love relationships, spirituality, moral values, dreams and goals. You could create a personal mission statement from the answers you give to these questions.

- *What kind of world do you want to live in?*

- *What part do you want to play in shaping that world?*

- *Why do you do this? What is your motive behind it?*

- *How will others benefit from what you do?*

- *If you did not do this, what positive would be missing from the world?*

- *What things makes you sparkle and feel alive? What activities do you love to do?*

- *What is the most exciting and fulfilling part of your life?*

- *If you were going to be recognized by others as a success, what would you want to be known for?*

All of the above should begin to give you a better sense of who you are and what you stand for. Your mission statement is designed to convey this. Once you have brainstormed, look for connections between the ideas, and decide what will be included in your statement. The purpose is to have something to use as a guide, to keep you focused on what is truly important.

Write your statement in a format that makes sense for you. You can write one flowing statement or break it down into the different aspects of your life. Beware of writing something too long, however, as you need to be able to recall your mission statement easily. Also remember to revise your personal mission statement – as you grow and expand, allow your statement to do the same. A mental conception of your personal mission statement is not enough. You must write it down on paper and put it up on your wall – ideally, where you can see it every day.

HAVING CONFIDENCE
IN COMMON SITUATIONS

This chapter focuses on developing confidence in situations that can often cause self-doubt and anxiety to flare: attracting the opposite sex, asking for a pay rise, making 'cold' telephone calls and competitive confidence. Emotional stakes are raised in these situations because rejection or a negative outcome can have powerful consequences upon a person's sense of self-worth when money, competition or relationships are involved.

Having confidence becomes vital in increasing your chances of success, because the greater the confidence you have in yourself, the greater the confidence you will cause others to have in you, thus increasing your chances of a successful outcome.

Going into these four areas with self-doubt and anxiety to the fore is akin to trying to cross over the border into another country without the correct currency or documents. Confidence enables you to be well prepared for the experience ahead.

I deserve success

I believe that I will succeed

I am confident and courageous

ATTRACTING
THE OPPOSITE SEX

It may be difficult for you to relax in the presence of members of the opposite sex, because you feel vulnerable and have a lack of confidence caused by the fear of rejection. Perhaps you are attracted to a person because they have something you need, so you perceive them in a position of power and yourself in a position of need. For example, you might perceive a potential partner as being a strong provider, having excellent social skills, or being a good home-maker.

The more attractive the person is to you, the more that is at stake, because their approval rating scores much higher. That is, your need for approval and acceptance on their part increases in direct proportion to how attractive you find them. If they reject you, the more attractive the person is, the greater the fall will be for you.

*their attractiveness + your
need for approval = anxiety*

FEELING GOOD ABOUT YOURSELF

The key to having confidence in this social situation is to feel attractive yourself. When you feel good about yourself, others will feel good about being around you, and you will become an 'attraction magnet'. Feeling attractive comes from engaging in what are known as 'flow' activities.

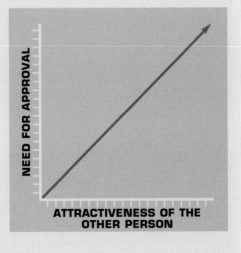

NEED FOR APPROVAL

**ATTRACTIVENESS OF THE
OTHER PERSON**

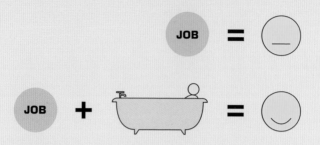

FLOW ACTIVITIES

What are the activities that make you feel really good about yourself? Some examples might be:

- *Going to the gym.*
- *Doing yoga.*
- *Playing sport.*
- *Going for energizing walks.*
- *Going dancing.*
- *Soaking in the bath.*
- *Having weekend breaks.*
- *Meditating.*
- *Singing.*
- *Making someone feel special.*

Discover what makes you feel good about yourself

Sometimes people stop doing the things they love to do because of external pressures, or because they don't want to appear selfish. For example, if you have a demanding job, it is essential that you engage in flow activities to provide you with the energy to handle the demands of the job. Without the flow activity, eventually the job will use up all your energy; few people who are slaves to their jobs find it easy to attract relationships.

So make sure that you pencil into your diary at least one flow activity a week, and schedule your other activities around your flow engagements. By doing this, you will guarantee that some time in the week is dedicated to you alone, a vital first step in becoming attractive first to yourself and then to the opposite gender.

INITIATING THE FIRST DATE

The key to initiating the first date is to discover what the other person's interests are, and then plan a suitable activity. For the busy professional, meeting for a first date over coffee or a drink is a good way to start. A nice, clean bar in a restaurant, or a coffee or juice bar with a pleasant atmosphere gives you a chance to converse and possibly plan another date. If the other person likes the unusual, then try rooftop views. Bringing your date to the highest point in the city can be exhilarating for both of you. Some hotels, restaurants or buildings have rooftop terraces for people to enjoy, especially at night.

THE FIRST DATE

Lots of people worry so much about the first date that they do whatever they can to avoid having one. However, once you have conquered a few first-date nerves you will find that the first date can be terrific fun. You are meeting each other for the first time and there is so much to discover.

The most terrifying barrier to developing relationships with women or men is learning to communicate with them. What do you talk about? Should you tell him or her about your childhood, your therapist, your plans for the future, your history of failed relationships?

'WHAT IF I CAN'T THINK OF ANYTHING TO SAY?'

The first thing to remember is that people often make the mistake of talking too much on the first date. They often monopolize conversations, droning on and on about topics that bore their date to tears. Very often, this conversational over-compensation comes from being nervous and the fear of the long awkward silence.

Keep in mind that if your date likes you, or would like to get to know you better, they will give you a lot of information to follow up on.

If they are not attracted to you, they will not give you much of anything, and it will be very difficult to maintain a decent conversation. No matter how charming you are, if they don't help you out you will eventually have to admit defeat and walk away. So be sure to listen for the topics they would like to discuss. Listening is an interactive activity.

As you learn how to communicate, the rest begins to come more and more easily. For example, as you are listening to someone, try to understand not just what they are saying but also why they are saying it. In order to converse for maximum attraction, you need to keep two other things in mind:

- *You need to tell them about yourself.*

- *You need to maintain a proper talk–listen ratio.*

The important thing is to show the other person that you are willing to drop all outside distractions and to focus on their needs for a while, and they will return the favour when it is appropriate.

Talk about subjects of interest to you both

INITIATING THE SECOND DATE

Before the date draws to a close, if you would like to see the person again this is the best time to initiate the second date. However, you need to determine the signals that your date is giving you. From their response, judge whether inviting them out again is feasible.

Warm response

If the date has enjoyed your company and feels warmly towards you, you can register this warmth in their prolonged eye contact, smiles, an easy rapport, the light touching of arms and hands, ready laughter and the sense of time passing easily. Tell them how much you have enjoyed the date, and ask whether they would like to meet up again. Keep the tone light and pleasant.

Cool response

If the date has been cool, this does not mean that they don't want to see you again. Don't be put off, as the person may be reserved and may want to spend more time in getting to know you. They may have recently left a relationship and may want time to find their relationship feet again.

Don't be overly pushy for the next meeting, as they might feel crowded. Give them

space. It may work best to arrange to call them. Make sure you have each other's numbers for a call or text message. You can send them a message after the date to tell them how much you appreciated their company. Their response will give you further clues as to your next step.

If they reply saying how much they enjoyed the evening, you can set up another date. If they don't reply, leave it a few days and then call them for a chat to see how they are. If the conversation flows on the call, invite them out on a second date.

Cold response

You can say the date was cold if the dealings were formal and stiff, with very little natural flow and rapport. Eye contact is minimal and conversation is forced with the distinct feeling of not having very much in common.

Ask yourself why the date was cold. Were you or the other person feeling under the weather, or did you really have nothing in common? Did you struggle to make conversation and bring them out of themselves? Was the venue less than perfect? If the date has not worked out, whatever you do don't be hard on yourself. Learn from it.

Avoid talking too much on a first date – it's a common mistake

> *Learn how to communicate and the rest comes easily*

SECOND DATE REJECTED

If they reject the idea of a second date, don't take it personally. Every date that you go on is fantastic experience in learning to develop rapport with the opposite gender. The rejection may simply be a sign that they were not right for you. From every date, something good comes. Capture the learning from the date and apply it to the next date.

What could you do better on the next date? For example:

- *Talk less about yourself.*

- *Be more relaxed.*

- *Ask your date more questions.*

- *Pay your date more compliments.*

If you are inexperienced in the dating game, it may take you a few dates to develop the right balance of confidence and relaxation. The date is the opportunity for you to show who you really are and to create an opportunity for the other person to do the same. With practice, you will be able to be yourself on a date and thus attract into your life someone else who likes you for just who you are.

PUTTING THE THEORY INTO ACTION

To be successful at initiating a relationship, remember to:

- **Discover what makes you feel good about yourself.**
- **Try to understand how other people think and feel.**
- **Tailor your first date to the other person's interests.**
- **Talk on subjects of interest to you both.**
- **Listen to your date.**
- **Be sensitive to their response to the first date when deciding how to follow it up.**
- **Learn from any unsuccessful date.**

ASKING FOR
A PAY RISE

Many of us fear approaching our boss to ask for a pay rise, because he or she is perceived as the person in authority and is seen to be more powerful than we are. Imagine that you have decided you are not receiving remuneration that is commensurate with your contribution, and that to address this problem you need to go directly to your boss to make your case for a pay rise. How do you build up your confidence enough to do this?

BUILD UP YOUR CONFIDENCE

Start by thinking about your contribution to the company or organization you work for:

- *The qualities you bring to the workplace.*

- *The success you have had in your current job.*

- *The pride you have in your work.*

GET YOUR TIMING RIGHT

First think carefully about when the best time to approach your boss might be. You don't want to ask for money the day after your company has made some workers redundant. Ideally, wait for good news. If you have recently had an argument with your boss for one reason or another, now is not the right time to push your luck either. You should ask for a pay rise only when conditions are right, both for your particular situation and for the situation of your company. Try to make your move at a time when profits are up, or just after you have finished working on a major project that made you and your department look good.

> *The greater the value you place upon what you do, the greater the value of the return to you*

EXERCISE: THINK SUCCESS

Add up the contribution that you make to the success of your company or organization, and decide what amount of money you think would be commensurate with this contribution.

Now imagine that pay cheque coming into your bank account. How does it feel when you think about this?

Savour the feeling of seeing this amount of money coming into your account. Enjoy the additional financial power this will give you. Delight in the treats you will enjoy with this extra, well-earned money. When you have fully savoured the feeling of this experience, make a small movement or gesture, such as clicking your fingers or scratching your nose. This gesture becomes your link to the desired state or feeling of being rewarded appropriately for all your hard efforts.

Do this exercise twice a day in the period before you go to see the boss. Just before you go into their office to ask for the pay rise, make the link or gesture that connects you to the feeling of receiving a healthy monthly pay cheque.

You are now emotionally prepared to set foot in their office, feeling a strong sense of value for who you are and what you do.

DO YOUR RESEARCH

Research salary information by finding out how much other people in your position would or do receive. Know how much you should be paid. If you can take any kind of documentation or maybe even a quote in with you when you approach your boss for a rise, that may prove helpful. Check newspaper advertisements or the internet, as well as simply talking to people, to find out how much you deserve to be earning.

DECIDE WHAT TO ASK FOR

Ask for more than you expect. This shows that you mean business and makes sure you are much more likely to get what you want. Say what you want to receive, but don't turn the discussion into a demand for money.

Don't be afraid to ask about benefits, such as company cars, as part of your negotiation

119

BODY LANGUAGE

Body language is crucial. Maintain eye contact with your boss, not with the ceiling, window or your fingernails. Don't fiddle with anything, so tie back your hair or leave off your watch if you have fiddling tendencies. Sit up and smile. Clothes also play a part in the impression you make. Dress as you want to be perceived. Sexy is not advisable, but businesslike is. Dress for your next position.

APPROACH THE SUBJECT

Have a basic plan ready. Focus on all your accomplishments, any new business that you have brought to the company, how you have made your department and, consequently, your boss, shine. Have you, for instance, put in a lot of overtime over an extended period?

DON'T SOUND DESPERATE

You are asking for a pay rise, so you obviously think you deserve one. Whatever you do, however, don't sound desperate. When you talk with your boss about a salary increase, talk as if you deserve the rise. Above all, never talk about any debts that you have, since this will make you come across as unprofessional.

PUTTING THE THEORY INTO ACTION

To successfully ask for a pay rise, remember to:

- Think positively about the contribution you make to the company.
- Time your approach to the boss accurately.
- Research and know how much your position is worth.
- Ask for more than you expect to receive.
- Talk as if you deserve the rise – don't be needy or desperate.
- Do the think success exercise.

MAKING 'COLD'
TELEPHONE CALLS

Many people in business have a tremendous fear of the cold call, particularly those who are new to running a small business and feel that they have to make cold calls to attract new clients. If you are a sensitive person, you don't want to offend or disturb the other person on the line. Perhaps you also fear being emotionally wounded by their potential rejection of your services. Maybe the receiver of the call will slam the phone down or speak to you abusively. When you are 'needy' for business, these rejections hurt, simply because you are desperate and very desirous of a 'yes' from the potential client.

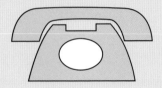

Confidence in this situation comes from the belief that you are going to succeed, whatever the opposition. It helps to stand up when you make cold calls, and have the attitude 'It's a great day – this conversation is going to be a success.'

PREPARING FOR THE CALL

Before you engage in a session of cold calling, prepare to build mental and emotional strength with this daily exercise. The well of strength is built by asking yourself certain questions that enable you to focus on the strengths and qualities you possess, so that when you make cold calls you have a reservoir or well of strength to draw power from. Typical questions would be:

- *What are the qualities that I bring to the job?*

- *What success have I had in my job?*

- *What positive things do my clients/colleagues have to say about me?*

- *What benefits will the work that I do, or the services that I provide, have on the person I am calling?*

GIVE YOURSELF A NICKNAME

Think also about what name or nickname you could give yourself to describe the motivation or reason why you do what you do. Here are some examples.

NICKNAME	MOTIVATION
The Achiever	You make things happen.
The Leader	You provide direction for others.
The Winner	You take on all challenges that come your way.
The Avenger	You want to prove a point to those who said you would not succeed.
The Provider	You want to support your family.
The Trailblazer	You want to push back the limits in your field of work.
The Team Player	You want to enjoy the camaraderie of others.
The Wealth Gatherer	You are working to gather financial rewards.
The Giver	You provide an outstanding level of service for others.
The Warrior	You want to be better than anyone else.
The Impresser	You want to live up to the expectations of other people.
The Inspirer	You want to make the world a better place.

Confidence comes from the belief that you are going to succeed

TELEPHONE TECHNIQUES

The first 15 seconds of any telephone call are crucial. One key to telephone success is knowing how to make your voice convey as professional a tone as possible. Here are some suggestions:

- *Use your natural voice pitch. Unconsciously 'switching' your voice to create another image is not only artificial but also harmful to your voice over time.*

- *Stand up when making the call: this increases your assertiveness and power. Smile as you talk – this releases endorphins into the body. Endorphins are the 'feel-good' hormones. You feel better and the person on the other end of the line will feel better.*

- *Notice the responses of your callers. Do people often misunderstand your name or ask you to repeat yourself? Do they hesitate when you expect them to speak? It is possible that they may not be able to hear or understand you very well.*

- *Listen actively. Let the person on the other end know that you are listening. Use positive responses such as 'Yes,' 'I understand,' and 'Certainly.'*

- *Know exactly why you are calling. This is essential. Be able to articulate your motivations clearly and concisely. This sounds obvious, but plenty of people don't handle this well and thus make a less than confident first impression.*

- *Know as much as possible about the company or person you are calling.*

- *Try to get a connection within any company before you call. If you can't make a connection, determine whom you are trying to reach (such as a human resources exec, a senior staff member or a particular manager).*

- *Be courteous and enthusiastic. If you connect with the person you were hoping to reach, ask if he or she is available to talk at that time or whether it would be better to schedule a later time to talk.*

- *Keep your responses short and to the point.*

- *Be friendly yet professional.*

- *Take notes (especially names).*

- *Be sure to follow up, sending any materials they request. Ask whether they prefer that you follow up by phone, e-mail, etc.*

- *Be sure to send thank-you notes after any substantial phone conversation (interview, information sharing, etc.).*

COMPETITIVE CONFIDENCE

This section is applicable to both sporting and professional situations where you are measured by your performance. The problem with this outward measuring system is that it can be highly damaging to confidence. It can lead to self-pressure and a feeling of 'I'm not good enough,' or 'I'm not as good as they are.' Almost every day we are required to respond to this way of measuring our performance. Confidence can plummet quickly, even though we may be trying our very best, so it is doubly important to retain a positive focus.

SPORTING PERFORMANCE

If you play any kind of sport, you may often find yourself in a situation where somebody asks you, in all innocence, 'Did you win?' or 'How did you do?' when you have finished playing. If your reply is 'No, I lost,' or 'I was seven over par,' then the tendency in these moments is to feel a sense of shortfall. You probably feel that in another's person's eyes you have failed. Perhaps you worry about what they will think of you. Maybe they exude an air of superiority that they did better than you, which serves to compound your anxiety.

PROFESSIONAL PERFORMANCE

The 'outcome question' constantly asked of sales professionals is 'How many sales have you made?' If you run workshops, the outcome question will be 'How many people attended the workshop?' If you are a teacher, your pupils' exam results may be judged. There are countless ways in which all kinds of workers are assessed on their professional performance.

POSITIVE REMINDERS

It is at these moments when we need a reminder that we are confident, and the exercise opposite is designed to enable you to connect to the 'already confident' you. When we are without confidence, we are afraid to try. Fear and anxiety impose themselves upon us. To be able to hold on to your confidence in the face of self-doubt, consider all the many moments in your life when you have felt proud, when you have had a go, when you have given your best without knowing the consequences or outcome of your actions. These could include passing your driving test, performing a concert or making a difficult phone call. The fact is that we must have been confident in those situations to have even tried to do these things – confident and even courageous.

You have had hundreds of confident moments

 EXERCISE: THE CONFIDENCE BOOK

Buy yourself a new notebook and begin to write down in it some moments in your life when you tried to do something new. It does not matter whether you succeeded or failed, it is the fact that you had the confidence to try that counts. Focus on the fact that you feel really proud of who you are and what you did. Your confidence lives in the ability to do. Here are some examples.

• 1970. School running race. Ran as fast as I could.
• 1988. Gave a seminar to business people on body language. Really did a thorough job.
• 1999. Gave up smoking. Required great self-discipline.

At the end of the week, read these moments aloud to yourself. Better still, ask someone to read them to you, ideally with a favourite piece of music playing in the background. The music creates the conditions that allow the emotions to be open, and therefore better permits you to receive the messages about yourself. Use the same piece of music each time that you do this exercise. The more you repeat this exercise, the stronger the link you will achieve between the feelings of confidence when you felt good about yourself and this music. After six months, you will be able to play the music without doing the exercise and it will cause you to feel confident and courageous.

Try to do this exercise every week for several months. Confidence underpins each of the moments when you feel proud of yourself, but self-doubt and criticism fragment this line of confidence. When this exercise works, it will reconnect the natural line of confidence that lives in you, and you will start to feel the natural, untainted confidence that you had when you were three or four years old.

CONFIDENCE-BOOSTING EXERCISE PROGRAMME

The daily exercises, tips and techniques provided in this programme are designed to allow you to implement all the ideas that have been discussed in this book. The purpose of engaging in this programme is to ensure that you turn the ideas into real confidence in your life.

THE 17-DAY PROGRAMME

DAY 1: MENTAL CONFIDENCE

DAY 2: PHYSICAL CONFIDENCE

DAY 3: SAY NO

DAY 4: TOLERATIONS

DAY 5: FLOW ACTIVITIES

DAY 6: THE LANGUAGE OF CONFIDENCE

DAY 7: SELF-ENCOURAGEMENT

DAY 8: DEVELOP WILLPOWER

DAY 9: PRACTISE FORGIVENESS

DAY 10: TRUST

DAY 11: SMALL TALK

DAY 12: BE IN THE PRESENT

DAY 13: SHOW APPRECIATION

DAY 14: REDUCE DISPERSION

DAY 15: ASK FOR WHAT YOU WANT

DAY 16: ACCEPT COMPLIMENTS

DAY 17: CELEBRATE

USING THE PROGRAMME

For real confidence to build and grow, you will need to implement these ideas on a daily basis until the new confidence habits and patterns become permanent. Don't do more than one exercise per day, to give space for the new habits and patterns to grow. Give yourself around three months to work through the entire programme. You may be tempted to stop the programme after a few weeks, once you start to have some success, but keep going, building your confidence foundations. The stronger the foundations that you build the more secure your confidence will be when it is tested.

DAY 1: MENTAL CONFIDENCE

How much of your time do you spend thinking about things in which you can do nothing about? Unnecessary worry can be very draining on natural confidence. Worry invariably leads to self-doubt, procrastination and inaction. Excessive worry causes the mental focus to be on what will go wrong rather than what will go right. A lot of worry is often about things that we can do nothing about anyway, or about things that are never going to happen.

 ## EXERCISE: RECORD YOUR THOUGHTS

This simple exercise is designed to help you get the mental clutter out of your head and free up your thinking for more confident decision-making.

On a blank sheet of paper, write down all your thoughts for 30 minutes. Don't censor these thoughts. Put down your darkest thoughts if they arise. Put down on paper the thoughts as they come into your head. Make sure that you complete the full 30 minutes. Write down everything that you think, then throw the piece of paper away.

If you genuinely find it hard to clear a 30-minute space in your day, start with five minutes to get the process moving, and then gradually try to increase the time you spend on the exercise.

(left margin, rotated)

Confidence-boosting exercise programme

DAY 2: PHYSICAL CONFIDENCE

Absence of confidence manifests itself in the way we walk and the way we carry ourselves physically. Naturally confident people carry themselves in a confident way. So it makes sense, if you want to increase your confidence, to carry yourself confidently. This sends a confident message both to yourself and to others. Observe the way that you walk.

EXERCISE: WALK WITH CONFIDENCE

A confident walk does not necessarily have to be fast. It needs to suit you and your physical body type. A confident walk could be relaxed and loose, or it could be brisk and upright with military precision. Experiment with both kinds of walk. The point of the exercise is to find a walk that gives you a feeling of increased confidence and purpose.

DAY 3: SAY NO

This day is for developing the habit of saying no with more confidence and less fear. To begin with, observe all the things that you say yes to that you would rather say no to. For example:

- *letting people walk all over you*
- *not complaining when you have received poor service at a shop or restaurant*
- *allowing others to put you down*
- *accepting second best from yourself when you know that you could do better*
- *getting drawn into criticism, judgement and gossip about others that you would prefer to avoid.*

EXERCISE: DETERMINE TO SAY NO NEXT TIME

In your notebook, make a note of those things that you have said yes to that you want to say no to next time. So, for example, if you have just let someone walk all over you, decide what you want to do next time this happens. Utilize the tips from Step 4 as you do this.

DAY 4: TOLERATIONS

This is the day to catch up with those annoying little things in your life that you have been putting off. When you deal with your tolerations, you develop the muscle to deal with things at the time they need dealing with, whether you like dealing with them or not.

Putting things off causes energy stagnation. For example, if you just vaguely think 'I must clean the rust from the car sometime,' you will probably never find the impetus to actually do it. Instead, say to yourself that you will do it on Tuesday. When Tuesday comes, because you have told yourself that you will do this job, you will be able to summon up the necessary energy and willpower.

Dealing with tolerations builds the habit of nipping problems in the bud before they grow. Whatever the situation, take charge and deal with it. If you don't, it will become more and more difficult to handle. The more tasks you don't do – after having said you will do them – the greater will be the build-up of unused energy within you, and this can lead to laziness, false promises and other problems. So dealing with your tolerations enables you to tidy up many loose ends in the background of your life.

 EXERCISE: DEAL WITH TOLERATIONS

Make a list of those things in your life that you are tolerating from:
- **your home**
- **your work**
- **your well-being**
- **your life balances**
- **your finances**

From your list, choose to:
- **do one thing about the house**
- **do one business/work item**
- **improve one aspect of your well-being**
- **deal with one financial item**
- **do one thing just for you**

home – change lightbulb in kitchen

work – request payrise

well-being – join gym

finance – work out budget

DAY 5: FLOW ACTIVITIES

For building confidence today, engage in flow activities. Flow activities, as described in Step 10 (see page 114), are those things that you truly enjoy doing. They are things you really want to do, rather than just feeling that you should do them. They are activities that leave you feeling energized and buoyant.

Many people fall into the trap of feeling guilty about doing things that they want to, for fear of being seen to be selfish. They have got into the habit of giving to others before they give to themselves. They may worry, 'What will others think of me if I do something for myself?' However, true friends will support you when you spend time on yourself.

EXERCISE: ENJOY A FLOW ACTIVITY

Choose one flow activity to engage in today, and set aside time for doing it.

DAY 6: THE LANGUAGE OF CONFIDENCE

Today is the day to choose a power word to use. A power word is a word that powers a quality that you want to build. In quiet moments during the day, for example, in a traffic jam, or in a queue, you can also consider confidence by thinking about the following:

- *Who are confident people?*
- *Look around – where can you see confidence in action right now?*
- *Where might you find confidence in daily life?*
- *What does it mean to talk to someone in confidence?*
- *What does confidence feel like when you have it?*
- *What does confidence enable you to do that you could not do before?*
- *Can you act in confidence, even if you don't have it?*

EXERCISE: USE A POWER WORD

If the quality you are searching for is confidence, then your power word today is 'confidence'. Write your power word down on a small card so that you will remember it throughout the day. Say the word to yourself. 'Confidence. Confidence. Confidence.' Savour its resonance. Using this method, you send a message to yourself that you are interested in developing this vital quality and are wanting to attract more of it into your life.

CONFIDENCE

DAY 7: SELF-ENCOURAGEMENT

Self-encouragement is an invaluable ally in building confidence, because it is a way of sending positive messages to yourself, rather than either sending yourself negative messages or waiting for others to tell you how well you have done at something. The best time to do this is before you begin work. Remind yourself of some of the qualities that you will be bringing to the workplace today.

If you don't know of any, or put yourself down so much that you don't think you bring anything to the workplace, then try asking four or five friends or colleagues what they see are the qualities that you bring to your job. Ask them to write them down anonymously on a piece of paper for you.

EXERCISE: ENCOURAGE YOURSELF

When you are clear about the qualities that you will be bringing to the workplace today, say them to yourself before work and at various times throughout the day, such as mid-morning, lunch and mid-afternoon, for example, 'Today I will be bringing the qualities of good organizational ability, punctuality, support for other people and customer service skills to the workplace.'

When you have finished your day's work, remind yourself of the qualities you brought to the workplace today.

DAY 8: DEVELOP WILLPOWER

Developing willpower is invaluable for confidence-building, as it puts more power and positive energy in the personal vitality tank for whenever you might need it. The absence of willpower leads to giving up easily, being put off by difficulty and not believing that you can succeed.

 EXERCISE: GO ONE STEP FURTHER

The task for you today is to choose one activity that you do regularly that you would like to go the extra mile with, as a way of increasing your willpower. Here are some examples:

DON'T BE PUT OFF When someone rejects an idea that you have, don't accept the first no, but use that no as an opportunity to discover more about what they really need.

COMPLAIN If you receive shoddy service in a shop or restaurant and feel dissatisfied, don't let it pass, but complain and let others know how things could be better.

DON'T WAIT If you see something that is not right, don't wait for someone else to act, do something about it yourself. You may be the catalyst for change.

TRY NEW THINGS Do a sponsored walk or some activity that enables you to go beyond your perceived boundaries of what you believe is possible and surprise yourself.

SEEK INSPIRATION Read stories of people who never gave up and still succeeded.

DO IT NOW Don't leave the dishes in the sink overnight, do the washing-up tonight and come down to a clean kitchen in the morning.

SET NEW TARGETS When working out, do a few extra reps past your targets, to develop the mental muscle of going one extra step.

START EARLY Arrive at the office 30 minutes before everyone else. You will get more done and make a positive start to the day.

DAY 9: PRACTISE FORGIVENESS

Today you will focus on practising forgiveness. Being able to forgive will help you overcome the negative habit of attaching blame to others and yourself.

EXERCISE: FORGIVE SOMEONE

The task today is to forgive yourself at least once and one other person or group of people. Try one of the following ideas:

• Forgive the driver who cut you up.

• Forgive yourself when you make a mistake.
• Forgive the waiter who spilled juice on your jacket.
• Forgive the person who turned up late for an appointment with you.

DAY 10: TRUST

Building trust between yourself and your instincts is invaluable. Trust is a vital ally in building confidence, because the more trust that you have in yourself the greater will be your ability to make difficult decisions and to do things that you have never attempted before.

EXERCISE: TRUST YOUR INSTINCTS

This simple and fun exercise should be performed for about 20 minutes. All you need is a matchbox and some floor space.

Take a matchbox and throw it onto the floor just in front of you. Now close your eyes, walk confidently over to the matchbox and pick it up. Don't rush or get impatient if you don't pick it up the first time. It may take a few attempts before you are able to collect the matchbox with your eyes closed, but keep trying and you will succeed. When you have mastered this exercise, close your eyes before you throw the matchbox. With your eyes closed, walk over to the matchbox and pick it up. This is a bit harder, but persevere and you will do it. Practise throwing the box further away from yourself and enjoy walking towards it with confidence. Don't worry about where the box is. Let your instincts direct you there.

DAY 11: SMALL TALK

Today you will concentrate on increasing your confidence in making small talk.

 EXERCISE: START A CONVERSATION

Initiate a conversation with someone you have never spoken to before, then see if you can keep it going for at least a minute by responding to the other person's statements with comments and further questions of your own. Any of the following general subjects could be used:

- the weather

- sports headlines

- world events

- popular music

- trends in fashion

- popular TV programmes

- office news

- local transport

Other ways of starting a conversation might be:

- asking for directions

- asking the time

- making observations about an incident you have both witnessed

- making a positive comment about something nice the other person is wearing

- remarking on the view

- talking about health, if at the doctor's or dentist's

- making comments in the movie queue about the forthcoming film

- if sitting in a café, commenting on the other person's choice of food and drink

DAY 12: BE IN THE PRESENT

Today the task for you is to slow down and try to allow yourself to become more present in each moment. When you are present and in the moment then you are not able to worry about the past or future. When you are caught up in a fast-paced, results-driven life, it is very easy to fall into the trap of focusing on the future. Being in the present means just that. All your senses are tuned in to each moment of your life as you live it.

One of the major obstacles to being in the present is the background noise that can go on in a person's life. Negative self-talk, worrying about the past and fretting about the future can all take us away from the moment, the present, where life is lived. The state of confidence is a quiet state, with no background noise.

 EXERCISE: FOCUS ON HERE AND NOW

To assist in reducing background noise, here is a very simple 30-second exercise that you can do anywhere.

STAGE 1: PAY ATTENTION TO YOUR EXTERNAL FOCUS
Focus on something outside yourself. For example, spend ten seconds focusing on something that you can see, such as an object in the room, movement outside the window or the pattern of the clouds.

STAGE 2: PAY ATTENTION TO YOUR BREATHING
Focus on your breathing for ten seconds. Take a nice deep, steady breath in, and then exhale slowly and steadily. Repeat this exercise a couple of times.

STAGE 3: LISTEN
Focus on what you can hear for ten seconds. Listen to the sounds around you.

• How many do you hear?

• Are they close in or far away?

• Are the sounds deep or shrill?

DAY 13: SHOW APPRECIATION

Today you will develop a positive outlook on life. Confident people are naturally able to see the advantages and opportunities in any given situation. Negative people tend to focus on how gloomy everything is.

EXERCISE: FIND THE POSITIVE

If, for example, you are at the dentist's, rather than having a negative mindset about the experience you could use the time to reach any number of new insights.

- 'I'm lucky to have teeth. Life without would be less pleasurable.'

- 'Without the pain of the drill, my teeth would fall out. Perhaps some other difficulties in life also help me to accomplish good things.'

Try to apply this positive approach today to a situation about which you normally have negative feelings.

DAY 14: REDUCE DISPERSION

Dispersion and disruption are a constant feature of our daily lives. Our concentration is constantly being interrupted by requests from others, by the telephone ringing, by e-mails arriving on our desktops or by somebody wanting something now. All of these interruptions lead to weaker and weaker concentration and less completion. This means that we are always trying to catch ourselves up, leading to self-doubt and the feeling that we can't cope.

EXERCISE: FOCUS ON THE CONCENTRATION

Set aside a certain time during the day for concentrating on one activity, and try to block everything else out. Make up your mind. 'I am going to do X for 15 minutes straight.' For 15 minutes, don't stop for anything that is not life-threatening. Practise this while riding on a bus or waiting for an appointment. Set yourself a goal of 15 minutes to focus exclusively on one subject. It may be a problem you are having at work, a personal goal or a relationship issue. The following week, increase this to 20 minutes, and after that increase it by five-minute intervals on a weekly basis.

DAY 15: ASK FOR WHAT YOU WANT

Unconfident people often find it daunting to ask for what they want. They fear being rejected and being perceived as greedy and selfish. Another common mistake is to expect others to know what you need and want, which, of course, they don't. Take a moment to reflect on the past week. Note how many times you have said what you did not want instead of what you wanted. 'I don't want to continue worrying about this.' 'I don't want to do this work any more.' 'I don't want to have to tell you again.' 'I don't like what is going on here.'

Not asking for what you want results in living a less effective life than you are already living. People who learn to ask for what they want tend to get better jobs, more money, less depression and less anxiety, and generally report feeling happier about their lives.

Asking for what you want does not mean you will get everything you ask for. It means you will get more out of life, and surprisingly more than you ever expected to get. When you ask for what you want, you actually tell others you are OK. Asking for what you want may get you some of the following.

- *A promotion at work.*
- *Your children knowing exactly what you want, instead of guessing at what is behind your request.*
- *Your partner no longer feeling ambiguous about what to expect from you.*

When you begin to ask for what you want from others around you, you will have clear communications and people will be able to trust you. Also, you will be getting more of what you really want and a lot less of what others want you to have. The energy generated by practising this technique will be obvious and rewarding.

 EXERCISE: BE VERY CLEAR

Ask for what you want at least once today. State clearly: 'What I want is ...' Invite those around you to ask for what they want as well. If something does not make sense to you, tell the other person you are not clear about what it is they want. When you ask for what you want, it is important that you continue to remember to say 'I' instead of 'you', 'we' or 'they'.

Practise this exercise and you will start to notice how much more you are getting, and how full of activities, money and positive results your life is starting to become.

DAY 16: ACCEPT COMPLIMENTS

Many people feel awkward when they receive a compliment or someone says something positive to them. 'You can't possibly be talking about me', they think, and dismiss the comment by changing the direction of the conversation. They tend to think that they are not worthy of the compliment and feel embarrassed. If you are like this, it is very difficult for others to compliment you. It is as if they are giving you a gift that you will not even open.

EXERCISE: ENJOY BEING COMPLIMENTED

Your task today is to accept any compliments that come your way. Instead of automatically rejecting any compliment, enjoy the moment and say 'Thank you.' In this way, the compliment will be received. The giver of the compliment feels good because they want to give to you.

You are creating an opportunity that allows both of you to win. They don't want their kind compliment thrown back in their face. Giving to yourself is as important giving to others, so start to develop this good habit by accepting the compliments that you are offered.

DAY 17: CELEBRATE

If you have had success with any of the exercises you have worked through on the previous days, today you should celebrate that success. Confident people are never slow to celebrate, because they have a natural appreciation of success and its worth. Celebrating success is a way of appreciating it and sending out the message that you want more success.

EXERCISE: MARK YOUR SUCCESS

Celebrate success by:

- buying yourself a gift or treat
- booking a holiday
- booking yourself in for a massage or other relaxing treatment
- taking time to be alone
- hosting a party
- spending time with your friends

The point is to make some kind of gesture from you to yourself that attaches significance to the success you have just had.

CONCLUSION

Congratulations on progressing this far! Rebuilding confidence and overcoming doubt takes no little courage and bravery. If you have completed the majority of the confidence-building exercises, you should now be a significantly more confident person from the one who first bought this book. Now you need to review the progress that you have made to date and clarify your next steps forward.

REVIEWING YOUR PROGRESS

Every month, it is a good idea to revisit some of the key insights and perceptions that you have learned from this book. Take a step back from your demanding life and remind yourself of what you want and what you need to do to achieve this.

Remember the advice in the introduction to work through the book with a friend. Having support is invaluable when you embark on personal development, because you are attempting to build new positive habits and patterns in place of self-defeating ones.

Support enables you to feel that you are not alone on the journey. Remember that confidence grows in the presence of warmth and encouragement, so make use of all the help that is available. You are not a lesser person for asking for help.

Building confidence comes from lots of small efforts all pointing in the same direction, rather than one big effort. There may be knock-backs and minor disappointments on the way, but the key to success is for you to decide that you will have confidence, and that you will not allow your life to be lived in the shadow of self-doubt.

Don't just hope for increased confidence or think that maybe you would like to be more confident. Decide that you will be more confident. Once you make that decision, you become committed to achieving that goal. Remember that confidence is there inside you at all times. Sometimes it gets overlaid by doubt, but your confidence has never really left you. It now awaits the chance to serve you so that you can live the best life that you possibly can.

Asking means you will get more out of life

INDEX

A

advertising 102
affirmations 108
Agassi, Andre 103
appearances 102
appreciation 105, 136
arrogance 12
asking for what you want 137
assessment tests
  comparisons 100
  confidence 8
  coping 70
  fear of failure 24
  saying no 42
  self-sabotage 58
  small talk 78
  speeches 90
attracting the opposite
  sex 113–17
  being stood up 60, 62
  feeling good 113
  first dates 114–15
  rejection 113, 117
  second dates 116–17
attractiveness 113
audiences 92–3, 98–9
authority 10

B

background noise 135
barriers, success 36–8
behaviours 107
being in the present 135
being the best you can 110–11
blame 16–18
  culture 28, 29
body image 102

body language 87–8, 120
bosses see managers
brain
  balancing left and right 97
  flooding 71
  mind/body connection 37
breathing 95, 135
bullying 9, 21, 44
burnout 71
Bush, George 98

C

capability 11
case studies
  audiences 93
  comparisons 103
  fear of failure 27
  fear of success 25
  motivational messages 63
  personal abuse 41
  professional footballer 23
  rewriting the past 39
  saying no 49, 51
  success magnet 66
  willpower 69
celebrating success 138
challenges 36
children
  curiosity 79–80
  learning 32
choice 43
Churchill, Sir Winston
  32–3, 95
Clinton, Bill 88, 98, 103
cold qualities 22, 44
cold telephone calls 121-3
comfort zone 24, 25, 40, 41

communication 115, 137
comparisons 100–11
  appreciation 105
  assessment test 100
  being the best you
    can 110–11
  definition 101
  influences 102–3
  self-encouragement 106
  thinking about others 104
competition 19–20, 124–5
completing tasks 64–5
compliments 138
concentration 136
confidence
  assessment test 8
  ecology 22–3
  examples 15
  exercises see exercises
  loss of 6
  magnet 15
  messages 63
  nature of 11
  notebook 125
  regaining 7
  spectrum of 12–14
confidence bouncers 55
confidence enforcers 9
confident people 13
  failure 35
  hallmark of 6, 110
conformity 18–19
conversations
  body language 87–8
  first dates 115
  questions 83
  revealing opinions 84

silences 85
small talk 78–80, 89, 134
starting 82, 134
coping 70–7
  admitting you can't
    cope 72
  assessment test 70
  distractions 76
  energy 77
  expectations by others 73
  procrastination 74–5
  relaxation 77
courage 48
criticism 16–18
curiosity 79–80
current affairs 81
cycle of confidence 10

D
dates
  being stood up 60, 62
  first 114–15
  second 116–17
deadlines 73
decisions 57
defective goods 52
difficulties 36
disappointment 20
dispersion 136
distractions 76
dominance 21

E
egotism 31
encouragement 17, 23
  self-encouragement
    106, 131
energy
  coping 71, 77
  drains 74
  stagnation 129
enforced confidence 9
exclusion 19
excuses 64
exercises 7

assertiveness 47
assessing yourself 14
being present 135
brain, balancing sides 97
celebrating success 138
clarity 137
compliments 138
concentration 136
confidence-boosting
  programme 126–38
confidence bouncers 55
conversations 134
examples of confidence 15
flow activities 130
forgiveness 133
imagining success 37
instincts 133
mental agility 96
moving forward 75
notebooks 125
positive approach 136
power words 131
reading 97
rewriting endings 38
saying no 56, 128
self-confirmation 106
self-encouragement 131
thoughts 119, 127
tolerations 129
versatility 97
voice 96
walking 128
willpower 132
expectations
  high expectancy 28
  other people's 73
  parents' 16–17
eye contact 88, 98–9

F
failure
  assessment test 24
  consequences 40–1
  dealing with 37
  fear of 24–33

interpreting 34–5
previous 31
fear
  confidence enforcers 9
  of failure 24–33
  of public speaking 90–1
  of rejection 34, 113, 117
  of success 25
  of telephone calls 121
  of unknown 26–7
feedback 35
flow activities 114, 130
forgiveness 133
friends
  exercises 7
  saying no to 50
  support 139

G
Gandhi, Mahatma 69
goals 36, 64, 66, 67, 103
golden triangle 10
gratitude 105

H
habits 64
  success 66
handshakes 88
happiness, self-sabotage 61
Harley Davidson 110
high expectancy 28
Hillary, Sir Edmund 32

I
imagination, success 37
inclusion 45
incompletions 64
inner confidence 10–11
instincts 18, 19, 27, 133
interruptions 80, 136

J
jealousy 104
Jett, Joan 32

K

Keller, Helen 69
Kennedy, John F. 95
key messages 94
King, Martin Luther, Jr 95
Kipling, Rudyard 33
knowledge 81

L

language
    of confidence 107, 130–1
    verbal mirroring 87
learning
    children 32
    from failures 35
listening skills 89, 135
loss of confidence 6
low self-esteem 14

M

Malcolm X 95
managers 17
    success culture 28
    tyrannical 9
    warm qualities 23
    work–life balances 49
mask of confidence 9
mental agility 96
mental power 57
mind/body connection 37
mission statements 110–11
motivational messages 63

N

names, remembering 86
negative influences 16–21
    self-talk 107, 108
    thinking 29, 37, 38–9
neutralizers 62
nicknames 122
no, saying see saying no
no-muscle 56
non-verbal messages 87
Norgay, Tenzing 32
notebooks 125

O

obstacles 36
opinions, revealing 84
opposite sex, attracting see
    attracting the opposite sex
outer confidence 9
over-protective parents 26
overspill 94
overwhelmed, feeling 71

P

parents 16–17, 20–1
    over-protective 26
partners 17–18
passion, speeches 98
pay rises 118–20
people, qualities 22–3, 44
perfectionism 20–1
Perot, Ross 98
personal mission statements
    110–11
positive influences
    messages 63, 131
    refusals 53
    reminders 124
    self-talk 107, 108
    thinking 29, 136
power words 108–9, 130–1
present, being in 135
presentations see speeches
pressure 73
procrastination 74–5
professional performance,
    workplace 124
progress, reviewing 139
promises 20
public speaking see speeches

Q

questions 79, 83, 99
quietness 10

R

reading 97

reference base 81
regaining confidence 7
rejection 34, 113, 117
relaxation 76, 95
remembering names 86
reviewing progress 139
Roosevelt, Franklin D. 95

S

Sanders, Harland D. 33
saying no 42–57
    assertively 46–7
    assessment test 42
    difficulties 44–5
    exercise 128
    friends 50
    mental power 57
    no-muscle 56
    personal life 48–53
    professional life 48–9
    rules 54–5
    shopping 52
    understanding no 43
    voluntary work 53
self-confidence 9
self-confirmation 106
self-destructive behaviour 107
self-discipline 76
self-disclosure 84
self-doubt 6, 7, 14, 34, 124
self-encouragement 106, 131
self-esteem 102
    low 14
self-image 59
self-importance 12
self-programming 60
self-sabotage 58–69
    assessment test 58
    completing tasks 64–5
    confidence messages 63
    definition 59
    neutralizers 62
    self-programming 60
    success magnet 66–7
    willpower 68–9

self-talk 107, 108
  fear of failure 31
  see also thinking
self-view 9
self-worth 112
sensitivity 45
shopping 52
shyness 79
silence 85
small talk 78–80, 89, 134
social conditioning 79
social confidence 78–89
  conversations 82
  listening 89
  making an impression
    87–8
  questions 83
  reference base 81
  remembering names 86
  revealing opinions 84
  silences 85
  small talk 78–80, 89, 134
Sorensam, Anika 25
speakers, great 95
speeches 90–9
  assessment test 90
  audiences 92–3, 98–9
  great speakers 95
  key messages 94
  overspill 94
  presentation skills 96–7
sport 124
strangers 79
stress 71
success
  acknowledging 67
  arrogant people 12
  barriers to 36–8
  celebrating 138
  common situations 112
  culture 28, 29
  fear of 25
  habits 66
  magnet 66–7
  self-sabotage 59

supremely confident
  people 13
support 139
supreme confidence 13

T

tasks, completing 64–5
telephone calls 121–3
Teresa, Mother 69
tests *see* assessment tests
thinking
  about others 104
  styles 97
  see also self-talk
tolerations 74–5, 129
touch 88
true confidence 10–11
trust 133

U

understanding 50, 110
unfortunate comparisons
  see comparisons
uniqueness 110

V

verbal mirroring 87
victims 44
voice
  projection 96
  tone of 88
voluntary work 53

W

walking 128
warm qualities 23, 44
wealth 109
willpower 68–9, 132
wisdom 92
work–life balances 48–9
workplace 17
  atmosphere 28–9
  cold telephone calls 121–3
  culture 28–9
  pay rises 118–20

professional performance
  124
  saying no 48–9
worry 127

Z

zero interference 11

Index

ACKNOWLEDGEMENTS

CONTACT THE AUTHOR

If you have find this workbook of practical benefit, you are welcome to e-mail news of your increased confidence to:

martin@martinthecoach.com

Alternatively, you can visit the author's website at:

www.martinthecoach.com

ACKNOWLEDGEMENTS

Executive Editor: **TREVOR DAVIES**

Editor: **KATE TUCKETT**

Design Manager: **TOKIKO MORISHIMA**

Design: **MARK STEVENS**

Illustrator: **DAVID BESWICK AT 'OME**

Production Controller: **NOSHEEN SHAN**